D1381202

T H E   B O O K   O F

FISH
& SHELLFISH DISHES

THE BOOK OF

FISH

& SHELLFISH DISHES

HILAIRE WALDEN

Photographed by
JON STEWART

a Salamander book

Published by Salamander Books Limited
LONDON

Published by Salamander Books Limited
129-137 York Way, London N7 9LG, United Kingdom

9 8 7 6 5 4 3 2 1

© Salamander Books Ltd., 1994

ISBN 0-86101-762-5

All rights reserved. Except for use in a review, no part
of this book may be reproduced, stored in a retrieval
system or transmitted by any means, electronic, mechanical,
photocopying, recording or otherwise, without prior
permission of Salamander Books Ltd.

All correspondence concerning the content of this book
should be addressed to Salamander Books Ltd.

Managing Editor: Felicity Jackson
Art Director: Roger Daniels
Photographer: Jon Stewart, assisted by Theresa Hayhurst and Brigid Land
Home Economist: Kerenza Harries, assisted by Amanda Clarkson
Typeset by: Pearl Graphics, Hemel Hempstead
Colour separation by: Scantrans Pte. Ltd, Singapore
Printed in Belgium by Proost International Book Production

ACKNOWLEDGEMENTS

The publishers would like to thank the following for their help:
Barbara Stewart at Prop Exchange, Unit F,
51 Calthorpe Street, London WC1

Notes:
All spoon measurements are level.
1 teaspoon = 5 ml spoon.
1 tablespoon = 15 ml spoon.

CONTENTS

INTRODUCTION 7

PREPARING AND COOKING FISH 8

SKINNING AND FILLETING 10

PREPARING SHELLFISH 11

FLAT FISH DISHES 12

FIRM WHITE FISH DISHES 27

RICH FISH DISHES 46

MIXED CATCH 78

SEAFOOD DISHES 94

SMOKED FISH 115

INDEX 120

COMPANION VOLUMES OF INTEREST:

The Book of SOUPS
The Book of COCKTAILS
The Book of CHOCOLATES & PETITS FOURS
The Book of HORS D'OEUVRES
The Book of GARNISHES
The Book of BREAKFASTS & BRUNCHES
The Book of PRESERVES
The Book of SAUCES
The Book of DESSERTS
The Book of ICE CREAMS & SORBETS
The Book of GIFTS FROM THE PANTRY
The Book of PASTA
The Book of HOT & SPICY NIBBLES-DIPS-DISHES
The Book of CRÊPES & OMELETTES
The Book of FONDUES
The Book of CHRISTMAS FOODS
The Book of BISCUITS
The Book of CHEESECAKES
The Book of CURRIES & INDIAN FOODS
The Book of PIZZAS & ITALIAN BREADS
The Book of SANDWICHES
The Book of SALADS
The Book of GRILLING & BARBECUES
The Book of DRESSINGS & MARINADES
The Book of CHINESE COOKING
The Book of CAKE DECORATING
The Book of MEXICAN FOODS
The Book of ANTIPASTI
The Book of THAI COOKING
The Book of CHILDREN'S FOODS
The Book of AFTERNOON TEA
The Book of GREEK COOKING
The Book of TAPAS AND SPANISH COOKING
The Book of CLAYPOT COOKING
The Book of VEGETARIAN COOKING
The Book of CHICKEN DISHES
The Book of WOK AND STIR-FRY DISHES
The Book of LIGHT DESSERTS
The Book of LIGHT SAUCES & SALAD DRESSINGS
The Book of CHILDREN'S PARTY CAKES

INTRODUCTION

Fish and seafood are very much food of the nineties, the epitome of modern cooking and eating styles – low in fat, high in protein, rich in minerals and vitamins, quick and easy to prepare and cook, and versatile enough to be adapted to suit any occasion. Plus, many fish are cheaper than meat and better value for money.

The Book of Fish and Shellfish Dishes provides a varied, eclectic selection of over 100 imaginative, attainable and attractive recipes for today's cooks. Many different types of fish are included, from plaice and whiting, to tuna and mahi mahi to mussels, lobster and oysters; suitable alternatives are given where appropriate. The dishes use a wide variety of cooking methods, including steaming, poaching, cooking en papillote, braising, baking and grilling.

There is a blend of new recipes and tasty versions of traditional favourites from around the world to cater for all tastes, budgets and types of meals, from Kedgeree for breakfast or brunch to Hot Fish Loaf for a family lunch, to Lobster with Basil Dressing for special occasions or Fish Cakes for a quick snack. Recipes are grouped according to the type of fish, such as flat fish, oily fish etc. The book starts with a helpful section of advice on buying, storing, preparing and cooking fish. Techniques that are used frequently, such as filleting or cleaning mussels, are illustrated with step-by-step pictures.

PREPARING AND COOKING FISH

Fish and seafood are valuable in a balanced diet as they contain more natural goodness, weight for weight, than any other type of food. They are high in good quality protein but low in calories; 115 g (4 oz) white fish such as haddock or plaice contain fewer than 100 calories while supplying up to half the daily requirement of protein. Even richer fish have fewer than half the calories of steak.

All fish are rich stores of essential minerals and vitamins; 'rich' fish such as herrings, mackerel, tuna, sardines and salmon are particularly good sources of Vitamins A and D. They are also very easy to digest.

CHOOSING FISH

Really fresh fish is easy to recognise as it looks bright and fresh with vivid markings. The eyes are clear, bright and slightly protruding and the gills pinkish or bright red (brown gills are a sure sign fish is stale). Skin is firm and bright with bright scales that adhere tightly. The flesh is firm and elastic and springs back when pressed. Any smell is fresh and clean with a hint of .the sea: exceptions are shark and skate, which give off a natural smell of ammonia, which disappears on cooking.

Fillets and steaks should feel firm, the cut surfaces look translucent rather than opaque, and they should not be dry or shrivelled. Avoid any that look slimy or have brown or yellow patches at the edges. If packaged, there should not be any milky liquid.

A lot of the fish sold in supermarkets, and some fishmongers, is thawed frozen fish. This has an unfortunate toll on its quality and limits its life. Thawed frozen fish should not be re-frozen.

Smoked fish should smell pleasant and smoky with no acid or musty odours. The flesh should be glossy and free from blemishes, and the colour even. There should not be any salt crystals, black soot or blood marks.

PREPARING FISH

The recipes in this book assume that fish has been cleaned and scaled; a fishmonger will do them for you if they have not already been done. Skinning round fish presents no problems, but skinning flat fish such as plaice is more difficult and you may prefer to get your fishmonger to do it for you.

Filleting is quick and easy after a little practice and providing you use a filleting knife. This has a flexible, pointed, straight-edged blade about 15 cm (6 in) long. With this type of knife you can feel round soft fish bones, removing every last scrap of flesh from them. A really sharp edge to the blade is vital for skinning, boning or filleting fish quickly, easily and efficiently. However, fish skin will blunt the edge of the knife quickly, so the edge will need frequent sharpening.

You will also need a heavy knife for removing fish heads, kitchen scissors for snipping away the fins, a large board and a clean, damp cloth.

Handle skinned and filleted fish with care and cook as soon as possible. Keep trimmings for making stock.

COOKING FISH

Fish and seafood should be kept cool in between purchase and cooking and should be cooked on the day of purchase. Fish and seafood respond well to all the healthy methods of cooking – steaming, poaching, baking, braising and grilling. These also preserve the nutrients and bring out the flavour.

Fish cooks quickly, but the flesh can dry out during cooking, becoming tough and disintegrating, especially when cooked by a dry method such a frying or grilling. To prevent this, fish should be basted frequently with oil, butter or marinade during cooking, or protected by a coating, such as yogurt, breadcrumbs, egg or oats.

When poaching fish, the liquid should remain at a very gentle bubble. Steaming is the most gentle method.

Choose the cooking method appropriate to the type and cut of fish. Delicate flat fish, and especially their fillets, need gentle cooking. Steaks of firm, rich fish, or sturdy whole fish, can withstand fiercer treatment.

The general guideline for whole fish or pieces of fish over 2.5 cm (1 in) thick, is to give fish 10 minutes for every 2.5 cm (1 in) of flesh measured at its thickest point. When poaching, begin timing the moment the liquid starts to bubble gently.

Acid ingredients such as vinegar, citrus juice or wine 'cook' fish, so if fish is marinated in a mixture that contains one of these ingredients, it will take less time to cook by heat; the longer the

marinating time, the shorter the cooking time.

When fish is cooked the flesh flakes when tested with the point of a sharp knife and will have just turned opaque. Flesh of fish on the bone will come away from the bone. To test tuna and swordfish, press the flesh – it will feel firm when cooked.

SUBSTITUTIONS

As fish and seafood are regional and seasonal, it is not always possible to buy the type specified in a recipe, but it is often possible to find a substitute, especially when fillets or steaks are called for. Below are some examples:

Plaice/whiting/flounder
Sole/brill/plaice/flounder
Brill/turbot/John Dory
Bream/John Dory
Cod/haddock/halibut/hake/monkfish
Red snapper/grouper/mahi mahi
   (dolphin fish)/bream
Pompano/pomfret/bream
Red mullet/bream/snapper
Tuna/swordfish
Mackerel/herring
Bass/salmon, especially steaks
   and fillets
Mussels/clams

── SKINNING AND FILLETING ──

SKINNING FLAT FISH

Flat fish are usually skinned before filleting. Lay fish, dark side uppermost and head away from you. Make an incision in skin across bone where tail joins the body. Working from the cut, loosen a flap of skin with a thumbnail or knife. Hold the tail firmly with one hand (a little salt on the fingertips or a cloth will help to get a firm grip) and pull the skin sharply backwards towards the head, not up. When you have removed the skin as far as the jaws, turn fish over and, holding it by the head pull the skin until tail is reached.

FILLETING FLAT FISH

Place fish with head away from you and eyes facing up. With point of knife, slit along length of backbone, from head to tail. Insert blade of knife between flesh and ribs to one side of backbone, next to head. With short, slicing movements, keeping blade next to ribs and at a shallow angle, separate flesh from bones. Continue working along length of ribs, following contours of fish's shape, until tail is reached. Cut fillet off at tail and trim. Remove other fillet on top of bone, turn fish over and repeat with underside.

FILLETING ROUND FISH

These are usually skinned after filleting: you will get 2 fillets from a round fish. Place fish on its side. Place point of knife beside dorsal fin, then cut down along backbone to tail, keeping blade just above centre of backbone, but close to upper bones of rib cage. Cut from dorsal fin to head end. Raise top fillet slightly. Working from head to tail, work fillet away from ribs with a slicing motion of blade. Slice along backbone again, this time with knife placed just below centre. Lift away backbone and ribs.

SKINNING FILLETS

Lay the fillet skin side down on the work surface and make an incision through the flesh across the tail end. With the knife blade, loosen about 1 cm (½ in) of flesh. Grip the skin at the tail end (a little salt on the fingertips or a cloth will help to grip firmly), slant the knife away from you and work towards the head, slicing through the flesh, very close to the skin, and pushing the flesh away with the knife.

——— PREPARING SHELLFISH ———

CLEANING MUSSELS
Wash mussel shells, scrape off any barnacles and cut off fibrous 'beards' protruding from join in shells; discard any cracked mussels or those that do not close when tapped. Scrub mussels under cold running water.

PEELING PRAWNS
To peel prawns, pull the head from the body, then peel the shell from the body, leaving the tail flange on if liked. For king (jumbo) prawns, make a shallow cut along the back with the point of a sharp knife and remove the dark intestinal thread running along it.

OPENING SCALLOPS
Give any shells that are open a sharp tap; if they remain open, discard them. Protect your hand with a cloth (and strong rubber gloves for added protection, if wished), then place scallop flat side up in the palm. Insert the point of a strong bladed knife between the shells near the hinge and at 45 degree angle to it (you may need to push and twist a little before it goes in). Twist the knife until the shell opens slightly.

Slide a finger between the shells then, with the knife in the other hand, quickly and carefully cut around top shell to free the muscle and allow shells to be opened completely. Push the top shell backwards to snap the hinge. Using a small sharp knife, carefully remove the greyish outer fringe of the scallop; do not damage the scallop. Slide the knife point under the black thread on the side of the scallop, then gently pull it and the attached intestinal bag away. Ease the scallop from the shell and rinse under cold running water.

—— BRILL WITH CARDAMOM ——

4 brill fillets, about 175 g (6 oz) each
250 ml (9 fl oz/generous 1 cup) fish stock
2 teaspoons cornflour
juice 1 large lemon
seeds from 4-5 cardamom pods, toasted and ground
2 egg yolks
45 g (1½ oz/3 tablespoons) unsalted butter, diced
salt and pepper
lemon wedges, to garnish
tomato, orange and spring onion salad, to serve

Preheat oven to 180C (350F/Gas 4). Fold fillets in half, then place in a single layer in a heavy baking dish.

Pour stock over fish, cover and cook in the oven for about 18 minutes until almost cooked. Transfer fish to warm plates, season, cover and keep warm. Meanwhile, in a bowl, mix together cornflour, lemon juice, cardamom seeds and egg yolks.

Stir a little fish cooking liquid into cornflour mixture. Pour remainder into a non-stick saucepan, then stir in cornflour mixture and heat gently, stirring, until sauce thickens. Remove from heat and gradually stir in butter. Season with salt and pepper. Pour sauce around or over fish, garnish with lemon wedges and serve with tomato, orange and spring onion salad.

Serves 4.

-STEAMED BRILL & VEGETABLES-

2 leeks, cut into fine strips
2 courgettes (zucchini), cut into fine strips
2 sticks celery, cut into fine strips
3 spring onions, thinly sliced
2 sprigs thyme
3 sprigs parsley
1 small sprig rosemary
salt and pepper
2 tablespoons lemon juice
4 brill fillets
2 tablespoons olive oil

Bring a saucepan of salted water to boil, add leeks, courgettes (zucchini), celery and spring onions.

Boil vegetables for 1 minute, then drain and refresh under cold running water. Lay vegetables in the bottom of a steaming basket. Add thyme, parsley and rosemary and sprinkle with salt and pepper.

Squeeze lemon juice over fillets, fold them over and place on vegetables. Add water to the base of the steamer, or a saucepan, and bring to the boil. Place steaming basket on top and steam for about 4 minutes. Discard herbs, season fish, drizzle olive oil over them and serve with the vegetables.

Serves 4.

Note: Garnish with fresh sprigs of herbs, if wished.

SOLE WITH MINT & CUCUMBER

cucumber, halved lengthways, seeded and cut into
   5 cm (2 in) fingers
salt and white pepper
4 sole fillets, about 175-200 g (6-7 oz), each, skinned
1 small shallot, finely chopped
175 ml (6 fl oz/¾ cup) fish stock
115 ml (4 fl oz/½ cup) medium-bodied dry white wine
175 ml (6 fl oz/¾ cup) crème fraîche or double (heavy)
   cream plus a squeeze of lemon juice
5 mint leaves, torn
25 g (1 oz/2 tablespoons) unsalted butter, diced
mint leaves, to garnish
mange tout (snow peas), to serve

Place cucumber in a colander, sprinkle with salt and leave to drain for 30 minutes. Rinse and dry well with absorbent kitchen paper. Fold fillets in half, skinned side in, and place in a frying pan with shallot. Add stock and wine and heat to just on simmering point. Poach for about 4-5 minutes, then transfer fish to a warm plate and cover to keep warm.

Add cucumber to pan, increase heat and boil until liquid is reduced by three quarters. Add crème fraîche and boil until beginning to thicken. Add mint, salt and pepper and juices collected on plate with fish. Simmer gently for 3 minutes. Remove pan from heat and gradually swirl in butter. Spoon sauce over fish and serve garnished with mint leaves, accompanied by mange tout (snow peas).

Serves 4.

—— SOLE WITH CHIVE SAUCE ——

115 g (4 oz/½ cup) firm cottage cheese, drained
   and sieved
grated rind and juice 1 lemon
salt and pepper
90 g (3½ oz) cooked peeled prawns, finely chopped
8 sole or plaice fillets, skinned
225 ml (8 fl oz/1 cup) fish stock
1 small shallot, finely chopped
1 tablespoon dry white vermouth
6 tablespoons dry white wine
175 ml (6 fl oz/¾ cup) double (heavy) cream or
   fromage frais or soft cheese
1½ tablespoons finely chopped fresh chives
prawns and chopped fresh chives, to garnish
broccoli, to serve

Preheat oven to 180C (350F/Gas 4). Oil a
shallow baking dish. Beat together cheese,
lemon rind and juice and season with salt and
pepper. Mix in prawns. Spread on skinned
side of fillets and roll up neatly. Secure with
wooden cocktail sticks. Place fish in a single
layer in dish, pour in stock to come halfway
up the rolls and add chopped shallot. Cover
dish and cook in the oven for about 20
minutes. Meanwhile, in a small saucepan,
boil vermouth and wine until reduced by
half.

Transfer sole to a warm plate and keep warm.
Add stock and shallot to wines and boil hard
until reduced by three quarters. Stir in cream,
if using, and simmer to a light creamy consis-
tency. If using fromage frais or soft cheese,
stir in and heat without boiling. Quickly pour
into a blender and mix until frothy. Add
chives and season. Pour some sauce over fish
and serve rest in a warm jug. Garnish rolls
with prawns and chives and serve with
broccoli.

Serves 4.

— SOLE WITH LETTUCE FILLING —

4 sole fillets
salt and pepper
squeeze of lemon juice
1 tablespoon medium-bodied dry white wine
1 tablespoon finely chopped white part of leek
85 g (3 oz) Iceberg lettuce, finely shredded
85 g (3 oz) ricotta cheese, sieved
1 egg white
lemon wedges and chervil sprigs, to garnish
beans and spring onions, to serve

Season sole and sprinkle with lemon juice. In a small saucepan, heat wine. Add leek and cook for 2 minutes, shaking pan occasionally.

Add lettuce, cover pan and cook until lettuce has wilted. Uncover pan, increase heat and heat until excess water has been driven off. Tip lettuce mixture into a blender or food procesor, add ricotta cheese and mix until smooth. Season. Whisk egg white until stiff but not dry, then lightly fold in lettuce mixture.

Place a quarter of lettuce mixture on one half of each sole fillet, then fold other half lightly over filling. Place fillets in a steaming basket or large colander. Cover basket or colander, place over a saucepan of boiling water and steam for 10-12 minutes until filling is just set. Leave for 1-2 minutes then, using a fish slice, carefully transfer to warmed plates. Garnish with lemon wedges and sprigs of chervil and serve with beans and spring onions.

Serves 2-4.

— PLAICE WITH PROSCIUTTO —

2½ large slices prosciutto ham
8 small plaice fillets
8 small sage leaves
2 tablespoons lemon juice, plus extra for seasoning
salt and pepper
1½-2 tablespoons light olive oil
15 g (½ oz/1 tablespoon) unsalted butter, diced
pasta, to serve
lemon rind shreds, to garnish

Cut ham into 8 strips lengthways. Lay a plaice fillet on each piece of ham.

Put a sage leaf at one end of each fillet, season with lemon juice and pepper, then roll up each fillet. Secure with a wooden cocktail stick.

In a non-stick frying pan, heat oil, add plaice rolls, seam side down, then cook until lightly browned all over. Transfer the fish rolls to a warm serving plate. Stir the 2 tablespoons lemon juice into pan and bring to boil. Remove pan from heat and swirl in butter. Season with salt and pepper, then pour over rolls. Serve on a bed of pasta, garnished with lemon rind.

Serves 4.

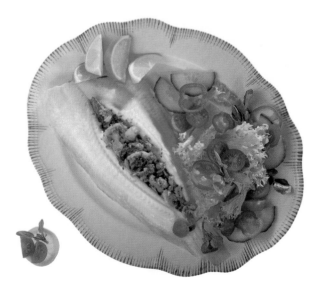

STUFFED SOLE

4 small sole, cleaned and dark skin removed
salt and pepper
1 tablespoon olive oil
1 small onion, finely chopped
2 cloves garlic, finely crushed
150 g (5 oz) mixed mushrooms, such as oyster, shiitake
   and button, finely sliced
55 g (2 oz) sun-dried tomatoes, thinly sliced
55 g (2 oz/1 cup) fresh brown breadcrumbs
1 tablespoon chopped fresh parsley
1 teaspoon chopped fresh marjoram
1-2 teaspoons anchovy paste or few drops
   Worcestershire sauce
mixed salad, to serve
lemon and lime wedges, to garnish

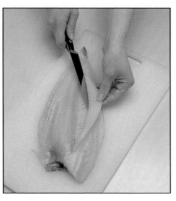

Preheat oven to 200C (400F/Gas 6). Butter
one or 2 baking dishes large enough to hold
fish in a single layer. Place fish skinned side
uppermost with tail pointing towards you.
Run point of filleting knife along line of backbone then, keeping knife blade firmly against
rib bones, slice carefully lifting fillet as it is
freed, until outer edge is almost reached –
take care not to pierce right through edge.

Repeat with fillet on other side of the backbone. Using sharp small scissors, cut through
the top and tail end of backbone and snip the
bones around the edges of the fish, taking
care not to pierce the underskin.

Insert knife point under one end of broken backbone and ease away from the under fillets. Lift up bone with the attached ribs and remove from the fish. Season fish inside and out with salt and pepper and place in baking dish.

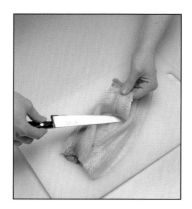

In a non-stick frying pan, heat oil, add onion and garlic and cook over fairly low heat until softened but not coloured. Add mushrooms and tomatoes and cook over a higher heat to drive off most of the moisture. Stir in bread-crumbs and herbs and anchovy paste or Worcestershire sauce and seasoning to taste.

Divide mushroom mixture between pockets in fish, cover with foil and bake in the oven for 10-20 minutes until flesh flakes. Serve with mixed salad, garnished with lemon and lime wedges.

Serves 4.

FISH & PESTO PARCELS

2 sheets filo pastry, 25 × 50 cm (10 × 20 in), total
   weight about 55 g (2 oz)
melted butter for brushing
2 fish fillets, such as turbot or salmon, about 150 g
   (5 oz) each, skinned
55 g (2 oz) cooked peeled prawns, finely chopped
55 g (2 oz) button mushrooms, chopped
5 tablespoons fromage frais or low fat soft cheese
2-3 teaspoons pesto sauce
salt and pepper
mixed salad, to serve

Preheat oven to 200C (400F/Gas 6). Butter a
baking sheet. Brush one sheet of pastry with
butter, place the other sheet on top and brush
with butter, then cut in half. Place a fish fillet
in centre of each pastry square. Top with
prawns and mushrooms. Mix together
fromage frais or low fat soft cheese and pesto
sauce and season to taste. Spoon a quarter of
the pesto mixture onto each portion of mushrooms. Reserve remaining mixture.

Bring together 2 opposite edges of pastry and
fold down over fish. Fold remaining edges
over and tuck ends under fish. Brush with
melted butter and place on baking sheet.
Bake in the oven for 15 minutes until
browned. Using a fish slice, transfer fish to a
warmed serving plate, split open top of pastry
and spoon in remaining pesto mixture. Serve
with a mixed salad.

Serves 2.

───────── TURBOT PARCELS ─────────

2 cloves garlic, unpeeled
2 large red peppers (capsicums)
2 teaspoons balsamic vinegar
1½ teaspoons olive oil
salt and pepper
8 spinach leaves, stalks removed
4 pieces turbot fillet, about 165 g (5½ oz) each
stir-fried mixed peppers, to serve

Preheat grill. Wrap garlic in foil and grill for 5-7 minutes to soften. Grill peppers (capsicums), turning frequently, until evenly charred and blistered.

Leave peppers (capsicums) until cool enough to handle, then remove skins. Halve peppers (capsicums) and remove seeds and white membrane. Peel garlic and purée with peppers (capsicums), vinegar and oil in a food processor or blender. Season with salt and pepper. Add spinach leaves to a saucepan of boiling water and cook for 30 seconds. Drain, refresh under cold running water, then spread out on absorbent kitchen paper to dry.

Season turbot, then wrap each piece in 2 spinach leaves. Place in a steaming basket or colander and cover. Bring base of steamer or a saucepan of water to the boil, place basket or steamer on it and steam for 5-6 minutes. Heat pepper (capsicum) sauce gently and serve it with the turbot parcels, accompanied by stir-fried mixed peppers.

Serves 4.

FISH WITH MUSHROOM CRUST

175 g (6 oz) chestnut mushrooms, finely chopped
2 tablespoons lemon juice
2 tablespoons wholegrain mustard
2 firmly packed tablespoons fresh breadcrumbs
3 spring onions, finely chopped
1¼ tablespoons finely chopped fresh parsley
salt and pepper
4 turbot escalopes or fillets, about 150 g (5 oz) each
lemon slices and parsley sprigs, to garnish
courgette (zucchini) and tomato sauté, to serve

Preheat grill. In a bowl, firmly mix together mushrooms, lemon juice, mustard, breadcrumbs, spring onions, 1 tablespoon parsley and seasoning to taste.

Grill turbot, skin-side up, for 2 minutes. Turn fish over, spread with mushroom mixture and pat it in.

Grill fish until mushroom mixture has set and fish flakes. Sprinkle with remaining chopped parsley. Garnish with lemon slices and sprigs of parsley and serve with courgette (zucchini) and tomato sauté.

Serves 4.

TURBOT WITH ORANGE SAUCE

4 shallots
115 g (4 oz) fennel, chopped
1 slim leek, sliced
small piece fresh ginger, sliced
350 g (12 oz) turbot fillet
2 saffron threads, toasted and crushed
juice 2 oranges
115 g (4 oz/1 cup) cold unsalted butter, diced
salt and pepper
orange slices and fennel or dill sprigs, to garnish
grilled fennel, to serve

Finely chop 2 shallots and set aside. Slice remaining shallots.

Put sliced shallots in a steamer base or saucepan with the fennel, leek, ginger and 450 ml (16 fl oz/2 cups) water. Bring to the boil, then cover, remove from heat and leave for 15 minutes. Transfer 115 ml (4 fl oz/½ cup) fennel liquid to a small saucepan and set it aside. Using a slotted spoon, transfer leek and fennel to steaming basket. Bring steamer base or saucepan back to the boil. Place turbot in steaming basket, cover and put it over the pan. Steam for 10 minutes.

Meanwhile, add chopped shallots to fennel liquid in the small pan and boil until liquid is reduced by two thirds. Add saffron and orange juice and boil rapidly until reduced by two thirds. Lower heat, then gradually beat in butter, beating well after each addition. Season with salt and pepper. Transfer fish to a warm serving plate, discarding leek and fennel. Pour over sauce and garnish with orange slices and fennel or dill sprigs. Serve with grilled fennel.

Serves 2.

—HALIBUT WITH COURGETTES—

350 g (12 oz) small courgettes (zucchini), thinly sliced
** on the diagonal**
4 halibut fillets, about 150-175 g (5-6 oz) each
65 g (2½ oz/5 tablespoons) unsalted butter (optional)
finely grated rind and juice 1 lemon
salt and pepper
4 sprigs chervil
lemon wedges and chervil sprigs, to garnish

Preheat the oven to 180C (350F/Gas 4). Generously butter 4 pieces of greaseproof paper large enough to loosely enclose each piece of fish.

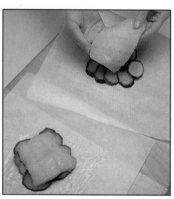

Bring a saucepan of salted water to boil, add courgettes (zucchini) and boil for 1 minute. Drain and refresh under cold running water. Pat dry. Make a bed of courgettes (zucchini) in centre of each piece of paper. Place a piece of fish on each bed of courgettes (zucchini). Place a knob of butter, if using, on each fish, sprinkle with lemon rind and juice, season with salt and pepper and top with a chervil sprig.

Fold paper over fish and seal edges tightly. Place fish parcels on a baking sheet and bake for about 15 minutes. Either serve fish and courgettes (zucchini) in the parcels or transfer, with cooking juices, to warm plates and garnish with lemon wedges and sprigs of chervil.

Serves 4.

——— HALIBUT WITH PAPRIKA ———

4 teaspoons olive oil
175 g (6 oz) shiitake mushrooms, stalks
  removed, sliced
salt and pepper
575 g (1¼ lb) halibut fillets, cut into
  1 cm (½ in) strips
1 onion, thinly sliced
1 large red pepper (capsicum), seeded and thinly sliced
2 cloves garlic, finely chopped
2 teaspoons paprika
1 teaspoon plain flour
pinch dried oregano, crumbled
115 ml (4 fl oz/½ cup) fish stock
115 ml (4 fl oz/½ cup) plain yogurt
rice, to serve
chopped fresh parsley, to garnish

In a non-stick frying pan, heat 2 teaspoons oil, add mushrooms and cook fairly gently for 5 minutes. Season with salt and pepper and cook for 1 minute. Transfer to a plate. Add fish to pan and sauté for 2-3 minutes until just cooked. Transfer to plate. Add remaining oil to pan, heat, then add onion, pepper (capsicum) and garlic. Cook until softened. Stir in paprika and cook for 1 minute.

Sprinkle flour into pan, then stir in with oregano and stock. Cover and cook for 10 minutes. Transfer half of pepper and onion mixture to a blender, add yogurt and purée. Return to pan with mushrooms and any accumulated juices. Reheat gently without boiling. Add fish and warm through. Serve on a bed of rice, garnished with parsley.

Serves 4.

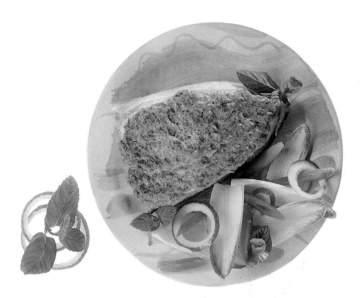

— YOGURT-TOPPED HALIBUT —

2 tablespoons cumin seeds
2 tablespoons coriander seeds
2 large spring onions, chopped
2 cloves garlic, chopped
2 tablespoons chopped fresh mint
2 teaspoons dried dill
150 ml (5 fl oz/⅔ cup) plain yogurt
1 teaspoon paprika
salt and pepper
4 halibut steaks, about 175 g (6 oz) each
mint sprigs, to garnish
red chicory, red onion and mint salad, to serve

Heat a small, heavy frying pan, add cumin and coriander seeds and heat until fragrant.

Tip seeds into a mortar or small bowl and crush with a pestle or end of a rolling pan. Work in spring onions, garlic, mint and dill, then stir in yogurt and paprika. Season with salt and pepper.

Place fish in a single layer in a shallow, heat-proof dish. Spread yogurt mixture over top of each steak, cover dish and leave in a cool place for 2-3 hours. Preheat grill. Grill fish, basting occasionally, for about 10-15 minutes until fish is cooked and a crust has formed on yogurt topping. Garnish with sprigs of mint and serve with red chicory, red onion and mint salad.

Serves 4.

CHOWDER

55 g (2 oz/¼ cup) butter
1 large onion, chopped
2 large cloves garlic, chopped
6 sticks celery, chopped
450 g (1 lb) potatoes, cut into small chunks
large pinch cayenne pepper
600 ml (20 fl oz/2½ cups) fish stock
600 ml (20 fl oz/2½ cups) milk
bouquet garni
225 g (8 oz) smoked haddock fillet
225 g (8 oz) fresh haddock fillet
115 g (4 oz) cooked peeled prawns
½ red pepper (capsicum), seeded and diced
115 g (4 oz) sweetcorn (optional)
salt and pepper
chopped fresh parsley or dill, to garnish

In a large saucepan, heat butter, add onion, garlic and celery and cook until beginning to soften. Stir in potatoes and cayenne pepper and cook for about 2 minutes. Add stock, milk and bouquet garni, bring to the boil, then cover pan and simmer for about 20 minutes until vegetables are almost tender.

Meanwhile, skin both types of haddock and cut into bite-sized pieces. Add to pan with milk and simmer gently for 5-10 minutes until fish flakes easily. Stir in prawns, red pepper (capsicum) and sweetcorn, if using, and heat through. Season with salt and pepper and serve sprinkled with parsley.

Serves 4-6.

— HADDOCK & PARSLEY SAUCE —

4 haddock fillets, about 175 g (6 oz) each
55 g (2 oz/4 tablespoons) butter
3 tablespoons lemon juice
150 ml (5 fl oz/²⁄₃ cup) fish stock
1 bay leaf
salt and pepper
4 teaspoons plain flour
150 ml (5 fl oz/²⁄₃ cup) milk
4 tablespoons whipping cream
1 egg yolk
4 tablespoons chopped fresh parsley
green beans, lemon wedges and parsley sprigs, to serve

Place fish in a frying pan, add half the butter, the lemon juice, stock and bay leaf.

Season with salt and pepper. Heat slowly to simmering point, then lower heat, cover pan and poach fish for 10-15 minutes, depending on thickness, until flesh just begins to flake. Meanwhile, melt remaining butter in a saucepan, stir in flour then cook, stirring, for 1 minute. Gradually stir in milk, then bring to the boil, stirring. Simmer for about 4 minutes, stirring frequently. Blend cream into egg yolk. Remove pan from heat and stir in egg mixture and parsley. Reheat gently, stirring, for a few minutes; do not allow to boil.

Transfer fish to a warmed serving plate, cover and keep warm. Remove sauce from heat and stir in fish cooking liquid. Discard bay leaf, then pour into a warmed sauceboat to serve with the fish. Serve with green beans and lemon wedges, garnished with sprigs of parsley.

Serves 4.

— HADDOCK WITH TOMATOES —

4 tomatoes
4 tablespoons virgin olive oil, plus extra for brushing
1 shallot, finely chopped
1 small clove garlic, finely chopped
juice 1 small lemon
1 teaspoon Dijon mustard
2 tablespoons chopped fresh chives
2 teaspoons chopped fresh parsley
salt and pepper
4 haddock fillets
chopped fresh chives and salad leaves, to garnish

Preheat grill. Place tomatoes not to close to heat and grill until the entire skin is blistered and lightly charred, turning them frequently. Remove charred patches and any skin that comes off easily. Halve tomatoes and remove seeds, then dice flesh. In a saucepan, heat 1 tablespoon oil. Add shallot and garlic and cook until softened. Stir in lemon juice and mustard, then whisk in remaining oil. Add tomatoes and herbs and season with salt and pepper. Keep sauce warm over a low heat; do not allow to boil.

Heat a non-stick frying pan and brush generously with oil. Add fish, skin side down, and cook for about 3 minutes until skin is becoming crisp. Turn fish over and cook for a further 2 minutes. Spoon sauce onto 4 warm plates and place fish on top. Garnish with chopped chives and salad leaves.

Serves 4.

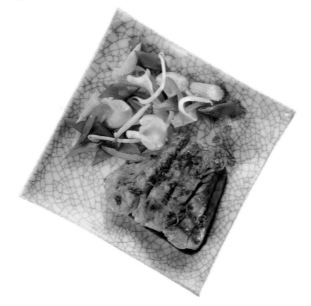

─COD WITH TERIYAKI GLAZE─

2 tablespoons soy sauce
1 tablespoon rice wine or medium sherry
1 tablespoon light brown soft sugar
1 teaspoon grated fresh ginger
4 pieces cod fillet with skin
chervil sprigs, to garnish
stir-fried vegetables, to serve

In a small saucepan, gently heat together soy sauce, rice wine or sherry, sugar and ginger for 2-3 minutes until lightly syrupy. Leave to cool.

Preheat grill. Grill fish, skin-side down, for 3 minutes, then turn fish over and grill for 3-4 minutes, until skin is crisp and flesh almost cooked.

Turn fish over, brush top liberally with sauce and return to grill for 1 minute. Transfer fish to warm serving plates and pour over any remaining sauce. Garnish with sprigs of chervil and serve with stir-fried vegetables.

Serves 4.

ROAST COD WITH LENTILS

3 tablespoons olive oil
3 shallots, finely chopped
2 cloves garlic, finely crushed
175 g (6 oz) green or brown lentils
3½ teaspoons crushed coriander seeds
300 ml (10 fl oz/1¼ cups) fish stock
300 ml (10 fl oz/1¼ cups) dry white wine
2 tablespoons chopped fresh coriander
700 g (1½ lb) cod fillet, cut into 4 pieces
pinch saffron threads, toasted and crushed
4 tomatoes, peeled, seeded and chopped
salt and pepper
coriander sprigs, to garnish

In a saucepan, heat 1½ tablespoons oil, add 2 shallots and the garlic and cook gently until softened. Stir in lentils and 3 teaspoons coriander seeds. Cook for 2 minutes, stirring, then add stock and wine. Bring to the boil and simmer for 25-45 minutes until lentils are tender. Stir in the chopped coriander. Meanwhile, preheat oven to 230C (450F/Gas 8). Heat 1 tablespoon oil in a non-stick roasting tin and fry cod, skin side down, for 2 minutes. Transfer to oven for 8 minutes.

Heat remaining oil in a saucepan, add remaining shallot and coriander seeds and the saffron and cook gently until softened. Add tomatoes, a little liquid from the lentils and season with salt and pepper. Cook gently for 5 minutes. Drain lentils and season. Serve cod on lentils, garnished with sprigs of coriander and accompanied by the tomato relish.

Serves 4.

FISH CAKES

450 g (1 lb) potatoes, boiled
450 g (1 lb) cooked mixed white and smoked fish,
   such as haddock or cod, flaked
25 g (1 oz/2 tablespoons) butter, diced
3 tablespoons chopped fresh parsley
1 egg, separated
salt and pepper
1 egg, beaten
about 55 g (2 oz/1 cup) breadcrumbs made with
   stale bread
olive oil for frying
lemon wedges and onion and avocado salad, to serve
dill sprigs, to garnish

In a saucepan, gently heat potatoes for a few
minutes, shaking the pan occasionally.

Remove pan from heat, mash potatoes, then
beat in the fish, butter, chopped parsley and
egg yolk. Season with pepper. Transfer to a
large bowl and mix well together. Chill if the
mixture is soft.

Divide fish mixture into 8 equal portions
then, with floured hands, form each portion
into a flat cake. In a bowl, beat egg white
with the whole egg. Spread out breadcrumbs
on a plate. Dip each fish cake in egg, then in
breadcrumbs. Heat a thin layer of oil in a
frying pan and fry fish cakes for about 3
minutes on each side until crisp and golden.
Drain on absorbent kitchen paper and serve
hot with lemon wedges and onion and avocado salad, and garnished with sprigs of dill.

Serves 4.

FISH GRATINS

½ teaspoon Dijon mustard
1 tablespoon lemon juice
1 tablespoon olive oil
pinch freshly grated nutmeg
salt and pepper
4 cod or haddock steaks, about 150 g (5 oz) each
85 g (3 oz) sharp Cheshire cheese, finely crumbled, or
    mature Cheddar cheese, thinly sliced
45 g (1½ oz) freshly grated Parmesan cheese
2 tablespoons fine fresh breadcrumbs
paprika
pattypan squash, to serve
basil sprigs, to garnish

Preheat grill. In a small bowl, whisk together mustard and lemon juice using a fork, then gradually whisk in oil. Add nutmeg and season with salt and pepper. Brush one side of fish with mustard mixture, then grill, coated side up, for 2 minutes. Turn fish over, brush top with mustard mixture and grill for 2 minutes.

Cover fish with crumbled or sliced cheese. Mix together Parmesan cheese and breadcrumbs, sprinkle evenly onto fish, then season generously with pepper. Grill until the top is golden and bubbling. Lightly sprinkle with paprika and serve with pattypan squash, garnished with sprigs of basil.

Serves 4.

—GOUJONS WITH PIQUANT DIP—

575 g (1¼ lb) firm white fish such as hake, haddock or
  cod, skinned
salt and pepper
1 egg, beaten
55 g (2 oz/1 cup) fresh breadcrumbs
olive oil for deep frying
lemon wedges and dill sprigs, to garnish
DIP:
150 ml (5 fl oz/⅔ cup) low-calorie mayonnaise
6 tablespoons plain yogurt
3½ tablespoons finely chopped gherkins (cornichons)
2 tablespoons chopped dill
1 tablespoon capers, chopped if large
2 teaspoons Dijon mustard

To make dip, beat all ingredients together,
pour into a bowl, cover and chill.

Remove bones from fish, then cut flesh into
thin strips. Season pieces, dip in egg then in
breadcrumbs to coat evenly. Half-fill a deep
fat fryer with oil and heat to 180C (350F).
Add fish, in batches if necessary so pan is not
crowded, and fry until crisp and golden.
Drain on absorbent kitchen paper, spear with
cocktail sticks and serve hot, garnished with
lemon wedges and sprigs of dill and accompanied by the dip.

Serves 4.

HOT FISH LOAF

45 g (1½ oz/3 tablespoons) butter
2 cloves garlic, crushed
¾ tablespoon plain flour
425 ml (15 fl oz/scant 2 cups) milk
575 g (1¼ lb) white fish fillets, such as hake or
   haddock, skinned and chopped
150 ml (5 fl oz/⅔ cup) double (heavy) cream
2 teaspoons anchovy essence
3 eggs and 1 egg yolk
lemon juice
salt and cayenne pepper
115 g (4 oz) cooked peeled prawns
2 tablespoons chopped fresh basil
lemon wedges and coriander sprigs, to garnish
cheese, tomato or broccoli sauce, to serve (optional)

Preheat oven to 150C (300F/Gas 2). Butter and line base of a 1.6 litre (2¾ pint/6½ cup) terrine or loaf tin. In a saucepan, melt butter, then add garlic and cook for 1 minute. Stir in flour and cook, stirring, for 1 minute, then gradually stir in milk. Bring to the boil, stirring, and simmer for about 3 minutes, stirring occasionally. Pour into a blender, add fish, cream, anchovy essence, eggs and egg yolk. Purée, then add lemon juice and season to taste with salt and cayenne pepper.

Spoon half of fish mixture into terrine or loaf tin. Finely chop prawns, then sprinkle them evenly over the fish with the chopped basil. Spoon remaining fish over the top. Cover terrine or loaf tin tightly with greaseproof paper, place in a roasting tin and pour in enough boiling water to come halfway up sides. Bake for about 1¾ hours. Invert terrine or tin onto a warm serving plate and tilt slightly to drain off juice. Garnish with lemon and coriander and serve with sauce, if wished.

Serves 4-6.

WHITING WITH ITALIAN SAUCE

3 tablespoons olive oil
4 whiting fillets, about 175-200 g (6-7 oz) each
2 onions, finely chopped
1-2 anchovy fillets, coarsely chopped
3 tablespoons chopped fresh parsley
175 ml (6 fl oz/¾ cup) dry white wine
black pepper
parsley sprigs, to garnish
orange, cherry tomato and spring onion salad, to serve

In a frying pan, heat oil. Add whiting and fry for 2-3 minutes on each side until almost cooked.

Transfer to absorbent kitchen paper, cover and keep warm. Add onions to pan and cook over moderate heat until lightly coloured. Stir in anchovies and parsley, stirring until anchovies dissolve, then add wine and boil until reduced by half.

Slip fish into pan, baste with sauce, season with black pepper and heat for 2-3 minutes, basting occasionally. Serve garnished with sprigs of parsley, accompanied by orange, cherry tomato and spring onion salad.

Serves 4.

— SESAME-COATED WHITING —

1 tablespoon Dijon mustard
1 tablespoon tomato purée (paste)
1½ teaspoons finely chopped fresh tarragon
squeeze lemon juice
pepper
9 tablespoons sesame seeds
2 tablespoons plain flour
1 egg, lightly beaten
4 whiting fillets, about 150 g (5 oz) each, skinned
olive oil for brushing
red pepper (capsicum), courgette (zucchini) and leeks,
   to serve
tarragon sprigs and lemon wedges, to garnish

In a bowl, mix mustard, tomato purée (paste), tarragon, lemon juice and pepper.

Combine sesame seeds and flour and spread evenly on a large plate. Pour egg onto another plate. Spread mustard mixture over both sides of each fish fillet, then dip in egg. Coat fish evenly in sesame seed and flour mixture, then refrigerate for 30 minutes.

Preheat grill. Oil grill rack. Brush one side of each fillet lightly with oil, then grill for 2 minutes. Turn fish over, lightly brush top side with oil and grill for a further 2 minutes. Using a fish slice, transfer fish to a warm serving plate. Serve with red pepper (capsicum), courgettes (zucchini) and leeks, garnished with sprigs of tarragon and lemon wedges.

Serves 4.

——WHITING WITH SPINACH——

1 tablespoon light olive oil
1 small onion, finely chopped
175 g (6 oz) button mushrooms, sliced
1 kg (2 lb) spinach, stalks removed
25 g (1 oz/2 tablespoons) butter
pinch freshly grated nutmeg
4 whiting fillets, skinned and halved lengthways
2 tablespoons freshly grated Parmesan cheese
salt and pepper
dill sprigs and shavings of Parmesan cheese, to garnish

Preheat oven to 180C (350F/Gas 4). Butter a
shallow baking dish. In non-stick frying pan,
heat oil, add onion and cook fairly slowly
until softened but not browned.

Increase heat, add mushrooms and cook for
2-3 minutes. Add spinach to pan and heat,
stirring frequently, until no surplus liquid is
visible. Add butter and season with nutmeg,
salt and pepper.

Spread spinach mixture in dish. Season
whiting, roll up with skinned side in and
secure with wooden cocktail sticks. Arrange
whiting on top of spinach mixture. Sprinkle
with Parmesan cheese, cover and bake in
the oven for about 20-25 minutes. Serve
garnished with sprigs of dill and Parmesan
cheese.

Serves 4.

MONKFISH IN COCONUT CREAM

seeds from 4-5 cardamom pods
¾ teaspoon coriander seeds
½-¾ teaspoon cumin seeds
generous 1 cm (½ in) piece fresh ginger, finely chopped
1 plump or 2 slim stalks lemon grass, crushed and
    finely chopped
salt and pepper
1 kg (2 lb) monkfish tail
2 shallots
1 clove garlic
25 g (1 oz) creamed coconut, chopped
150 ml (5 fl oz/⅔ cup) hot water
Chinese noodles, baby corn and baby courgettes
    (zucchini), to garnish
lemon slices, to garnish

Preheat oven to 180C (350F/Gas 4). Heat a
heavy pan, add cardamom, coriander and
cumin seeds and heat until fragrant. Tip into
a mortar or small bowl and crush finely with
pestle or end of a rolling pin. Crush in ginger,
lemon grass and pepper. Remove fine skin
and the bone from monkfish, cut flesh into
4 pieces and rub spice mixture into them.
Leave for 30 minutes.

Finely chop shallots and garlic together and
put half in a shallow baking dish just large
enough to hold fish. Place fish on shallot
mixture and scatter remaining mixture over
the top. Blend coconut with water until
smooth, then pour it over fish. Season with
salt and pepper, then cover and bake for
about 30 minutes. Serve with Chinese
noodles, sliced baby corn and courgettes
(zucchini), garnished with lemon slices.

Serves 4.

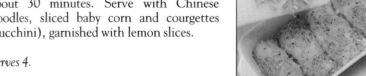

—MIDDLE EASTERN MONKFISH—

2 cloves garlic
6.25 cm (2½ in) piece fresh ginger
3 tablespoons olive oil
2½ tablespoons tomato purée (paste)
1½ teaspoons ground cinnamon
1 teaspoon caraway seeds, crushed
salt and pepper
1 kg (2 lb) monkfish tail
½ Spanish onion, finely chopped
cous cous and lemon slices, to serve

Finely chop garlic and ginger together. In a small bowl, stir oil into tomato purée (paste), then stir in ginger and garlic, cinnamon and caraway seeds. Season with salt and pepper.

Remove fine skin from monkfish, then spread with spice mixture. Place fish in a shallow dish, cover and leave in a cool place for 1-1½ hours.

Preheat oven to 200C (400F/Gas 6). Cut a piece of foil large enough to enclose fish. Make a bed of chopped onion on foil and place monkfish, and any spice paste left in dish, on onion. Fold foil loosely over fish and seal edges tightly. Bake monkfish for 20-25 minutes. Open foil, baste fish and bake for a further 10-15 minutes. Serve on a bed of cous cous, garnished with lemon slices.

Serves 4.

──CHUNKY FISH CASSEROLE──

100 g (3½ oz) pasta shells
3 tablespoons olive oil
2 cloves garlic, finely crushed
85 g (3 oz) button onions, halved
115 g (4 oz) button mushrooms, halved
450 g (1 lb) firm, white fish, such as cod or monkfish
225 g (8 oz) trout fillets
3 tablespoons well-seasoned plain flour
225 g (8 oz) broad beans
115 ml (4 fl oz/½ cup) dry white wine
300 ml (10 fl oz/1¼ cups) fish stock
large bouquet garni
grated rind and juice 1 lemon
150 g (5 oz) cooked peeled prawns or cooked shelled
    mussels or clams
chopped fresh herbs, to garnish

Preheat oven to 180C (350F/Gas 4). Cook pasta in plenty of boiling salted water for three quarters of time recommended on packet. Drain and rinse under cold running water; set aside. In a large frying pan, heat half the oil, add garlic, onions and mushrooms and cook for 3-4 minutes. Using a slotted spoon, transfer to a large, deep baking dish. Meanwhile, skin fish and cut into 2.5 cm (1 in) chunks, then toss in seasoned flour.

Add remaining oil to pan, heat and then add fish, in batches if necessary. Fry for 2-3 minutes, turning pieces carefully. Transfer to dish and add pasta and beans. Stir wine, stock, bouquet garni and lemon rind and juice into pan and bring to the boil. Simmer for a few minutes, then pour into dish. Cover and cook in oven for about 30 minutes. Add prawns, mussels or clams, cover again and cook for about 5 minutes. Garnish with plenty of chopped herbs.

Serves 4.

—MONKFISH ON RATATOUILLE—

2 aubergines (eggplants), halved lengthways
3 courgettes (zucchini), sliced
salt and pepper
2 monkfish tails, total weight about 1.15 kg (2½ lb)
6 cloves garlic
5 tablespoons olive oil
1 Spanish onion, very thinly sliced
2 large red peppers (capsicums), thinly sliced
4 large tomatoes, skinned, seeded and chopped
leaves from a few sprigs of thyme, marjoram and
    oregano
about 2 tablespoons each chopped parsley and torn basil

Cut aubergines (eggplants) into 2.5 cm (1 in) slices. Put into a colander with courgette (zucchini) slices, sprinkle with salt and leave for 1 hour. Rinse well, then dry thoroughly with absorbent kitchen paper.

Meanwhile, remove fine skin from monkfish and cut slits in flesh. Cut 3 garlic cloves into thin slivers and insert in slits. Season with salt and pepper and set aside. Chop remaining garlic.

In a heavy flameproof casserole, heat 2 tablespoons oil, add aubergine (eggplant) slices and sauté for a few minutes. Add another tablespoon oil and the onion and garlic and sauté for a few minutes. Add peppers (capsicums) and cook for 1 minute, stirring occasionally.

Add 2 more tablespoons oil and the courgettes (zucchini). Stir occasionally for a few minutes, then add tomatoes, snip in herb leaves and season lightly. Cover and cook very gently for 30-40 minutes, stirring occasionally until fairly dry.

Preheat oven to 200C (400F/Gas 6). Stir parsley into ratatouille and tip into a baking dish. Lay monkfish on top and cook for 30-40 minutes, turning fish occasionally. Sprinkle with basil just before end of cooking.

Serves 4-6.

CEVICHE

450 g (1 lb) monkfish or halibut fillets, thinly sliced
1 fresh red chilli, seeded and thinly sliced
2 teaspoons coriander seeds, toasted and finely crushed
salt
juice 4 limes
2½ tablespoons virgin olive oil
½ red onion, thinly sliced
1 beefsteak tomato, peeled, seeded and cut into
    thin strips
1 red pepper (capsicum), seeded and chopped
1 tablespoon chopped fresh coriander
lime wedges, to garnish
lamb's lettuce and red chicory salad, to serve

Lay fish in a shallow, non-metallic dish. Scatter over chilli and coriander seeds and sprinkle with salt. Pour over lime juice. Cover and leave at room temperature for 1 hour, or 2-4 hours in refrigerator.

Drain off juices from fish and mix 2½ table-spoons with the oil; discard remaining juices. Scatter onion, tomato, pepper (capsicum) and chopped coriander over fish. Trickle oil mixture over the vegetables and fish. Serve garnished with lime wedges and accompanied by lamb's lettuce and red chicory salad.

Serves 4 for a first course.

—GRILLED FISH & CORIANDER—

700 g (1½ lb) grey mullet, bream or monkfish fillets
3 tablespoons olive oil
2 cloves garlic, crushed
1½ teaspoons ground toasted cumin seeds
1 teaspoon paprika
1 fresh green chilli, finely chopped
handful coriander leaves, finely chopped
3 tablespoons lime juice
salt
rice, to serve
mint sprigs and lime wedges, to serve

Place fish in a shallow, non-metallic dish. Mix together remaining ingredients, except rice, mint and lime wedges.

Spoon olive oil mixture over fish, cover and leave in a cool place for 3-4 hours, turning occasionally.

Preheat grill. Grill fish for about 4 minutes on each side, basting with coriander mixture occasionally, until flesh flakes when tested with the point of a sharp knife. Serve warm on a bed of rice, garnished with sprigs of mint and lime wedges.

Serves 4.

– HAKE BAKED WITH POTATOES –

450 g (1 lb) yellow potatoes, very thinly sliced, rinsed
  and dried
1 red pepper (capsicum), cored and seeded
1 onion, thinly sliced
1 large tomato, chopped
3 cloves garlic, slivered
4 tablespoons chopped fresh parsley
salt and pepper
225 ml (8 fl oz/1 cup) fish stock (optional)
700 g (1½ lb) hake cutlets with skin, 2.5 cm (1 in) thick
1 bay leaf
3 sprigs thyme
4 thin slices lemon
1 tablespoon olive oil
4 tablespoons dry sherry
oregano sprigs, to garnish

Preheat oven to 190C (375F/Gas 5). Place
half the potato slices in a large, lightly oiled
baking dish. Chop pepper (capsicum), then
scatter it over potatoes with onion, tomato,
garlic and parsley. Season with salt and
pepper and cover with remaining potato
slices. Pour over stock, or 225 ml (8 fl oz/
1 cup) water, cover dish and bake in the oven
for 1 hour. Increase oven temperature to
220C (425F/Gas 7), uncover dish and bake
for about 7 minutes.

Season fish. Place bay leaf and 3 sprigs of
thyme on potatoes, then place fish on top and
nestle it into potatoes. Lay lemon slices on
fish, trickle oil over the top and return to
oven for 8 minutes until potatoes are crisp
and brown. Pour sherry over fish and return
to oven for 2 minutes. Serve garnished with
sprigs of oregano.

Serves 4.

– RED SNAPPER WITH CROSTINI –

4 red snapper or red mullet fillets
4½ tablespoons olive oil
5 black peppercorns, coarsely crushed
1 orange, peeled and thinly sliced
juice 1 lemon
1 small fennel bulb, quartered
salt and pepper
8 thin slices French bread
2 cloves garlic, cut in half
3-4 anchovy fillets
juice ½ orange
fennel sprigs and orange slices, to garnish

Prick fish with a skewer, then lay them in a single layer in a shallow, non-metallic dish.

Pour over 2½ tablespoons olive oil. Add peppercorns and orange slices. Cover and leave in the bottom of the refrigerator, or other cool place, for 8 hours, turning occasionally. In a small saucepan of boiling water with the lemon juice added, cook fennel until soft. Drain fennel, then purée with ½ tablespoon olive oil in a food processor or blender. Season with salt and pepper and keep warm. Rub bread with cut surfaces of garlic, then fry in remaining olive oil. Keep warm.

Drain fish and reserve marinade. In a frying pan, fry fish in 1½ tablespoons marinade for about 3 minutes each side. Transfer to a warm plate and keep warm. Add anchovies to pan, crushing them into the oil, then add orange juice and heat through. Season with pepper, then pour it over the fish. Spread fennel purée on the bread and serve with fish. Garnish with sprigs of fennel and orange slices.

Serves 2-4.

—— BREAM WITH TARRAGON ——

2 tablespoons white wine vinegar
1 ½-2 teaspoons Dijon mustard
1 small shallot, finely chopped
1 clove garlic, finely crushed
115 ml (4 fl oz/½ cup) olive oil, plus extra for brushing
400 g (14 oz) tomatoes, peeled, seeded and diced
1 ½ tablespoons chopped fresh tarragon
2 tablespoons finely chopped fresh chives
salt and pepper
pinch caster sugar (optional)
4 red bream or red mullet, about 300 g (10 oz) each, scaled
4 sprigs tarragon
tarragon sprigs and lime wedges, to garnish

Whisk together vinegar, mustard, shallot and garlic until mixture is emulsified, then gradually whisk in oil. Add tomatoes, tarragon and chives and season with salt and pepper. Add a pinch of sugar, if wished, then leave to stand for 30-60 minutes.

Preheat grill. With the point of a sharp knife, cut 2 slashes on each side of the fish. Season fish, put a tarragon sprig in each cavity and brush with oil, then grill for 10-11 minutes, turning and brushing with oil once. Transfer to serving plates. Stir tomato mixture, spoon some on to fish and serve remainder separately. Garnish with sprigs of tarragon and lime wedges.

Serves 4.

SEA BASS UNDER A CRUST

1 kg (2 lb) sea bass, cleaned but not scaled,
   fins trimmed
4-5 herb sprigs, such as tarragon, basil, fennel and
   parsley
5 crushed black peppercorns
2 kg (4 lb) coarse sea salt
tomato, basil, red onion and caper salad, to serve
lemon wedges and basil sprigs, to garnish

Preheat oven to 220C (425F/Gas 7). Place herb sprigs and a few peppercorns in cavity of sea bass. Spread a layer of salt about 2.5 cm (1 in) deep in a deep baking dish that the fish will fit without too much space around.

Place fish on the salt, then pack salt around it until fish is completely buried and there is a 2.5 cm (1 in) layer on top. Bake fish in the oven for about 25 minutes.

To serve, crack open salt crust and remove pieces carefully to expose whole fish. Remove skin from top of fish and serve the fish with tomato, basil, red onion and caper salad, garnished with lemon wedges and sprigs of basil.

Serves 2-3.

SEA BASS & GARLIC

20 g (¾ oz/1½ tablespoons) unsalted butter
8 cloves garlic, with skin, lightly crushed
16 spring onions, cut into slices
4 sea bass fillets with skin, about 200 g (7 oz) each
salt and pepper
2 slices lean smoked bacon, cut into thin strips
1 sprig thyme
115 ml (4 fl oz/½ cup) fish stock
1 tablespoon chopped fresh parsley
tarragon sprigs, to garnish
new potatoes, to serve

Preheat oven to 200C (400F/Gas 6). In a heavy, shallow flameproof casserole, heat butter, add garlic and spring onions and cook slowly until browned. Season skin side of fish, then add, skin side down, to casserole with bacon and thyme. Cook for about 2 minutes, turn fish over and add stock.

Place casserole in oven for 4-6 minutes. Stir in parsley, and add seasoning if necessary. Garnish with sprigs of tarragon and serve with new potatoes.

Serves 4.

—BASS WITH GINGER & LIME—

2 shallots, finely chopped
4 cm (1½ in) piece fresh ginger, finely chopped
juice 2 limes
4 tablespoons rice wine vinegar
225 ml (8 fl oz/1 cup) olive oil
2 tablespoons Chinese sesame oil
2 tablespoons soy sauce
salt and pepper
6-8 bass fillets, about 175 g (6 oz) and 1 cm (½ in)
    thick each
leaves from 1 bunch coriander
toasted sesame seeds, to garnish
stir-fried baby corn and sun-dried tomatoes, to serve

In a bowl, mix together first 8 ingredients. Set aside.

Preheat grill. Brush fish lightly with ginger mixture, then grill under a high heat for 2-3 minutes on each side.

Just before serving, reserve a few coriander leaves for garnish, chop remainder and mix into ginger mixture. Spoon some onto serving plates at room temperature and place fish on top. Sprinkle with sesame seeds and garnish with reserved coriander. Serve with stir-fried baby corn and sun-dried tomatoes.

Serves 6-8.

SPICED BASS

4 bass steaks, about 150-175 g (5-6 oz) each
courgette (zucchini) and spring onion salad, to serve
lemon rind and coriander sprigs, to garnish
MARINADE:
1 cm (½ in) piece fresh ginger
1 clove garlic
2 spring onions, sliced
1 tablespoon lime juice
1 tablespoon sesame oil
2 tablespoons grapeseed oil
½ teaspoon Chinese five spice powder
2 tablespoons sake or dry sherry

To make marinade, mix ginger, garlic, spring
onions and lime juice to a paste in a blender.
With motor running, slowly pour in oils,
then add five spice powder and sake or sherry.

Put bass in a single layer in a non-metallic
dish, pour over marinade, then leave for
1 hour. Preheat grill. Remove fish from
marinade and grill for about 4 minutes on
each side, brushing with marinade when fish
is turned. Serve with courgette (zucchini)
and spring onion salad, garnished with lemon
rind and sprigs of coriander.

Serves 4.

– TROUT WITH TOMATO SAUCE –

65 g (2½ oz) sun-dried tomatoes
2 teaspoons capers
1 large clove garlic, crushed
8 basil leaves
leaves from 2 small sprigs rosemary
leaves from 2 sprigs oregano
55 g (2 oz/¼ cup) butter, plus extra for brushing
1 tablespoon crème fraîche or sour cream
300 ml (10 fl oz/1¼ cups) fish stock
salt and pepper
6-8 trout fillets
sugar snap peas and sun-dried tomatoes, to serve
lemon wedges and oregano sprigs, to garnish

In a blender or food processor, mix together sun-dried tomatoes, capers, garlic, herbs, butter, crème fraîche and stock until smooth. Season with pepper and just a little salt. Pour into a saucepan.

Preheat grill. Brush trout with butter, season with pepper, then grill for 3-4 minutes on each side. Meanwhile, heat sauce gently, stirring occasionally. Transfer fish to warm plates, season with salt and spoon the sauce over the fish. Serve with sugar snap peas and sun-dried tomatoes, garnished with lemon wedges and sprigs of oregano.

Serves 3-4.

—TROUT WITH HAZELNUTS—

115 g (4 oz/²/₃ cup) hazelnuts in their shells
65 g (2½ oz/5 tablespoons) butter
4 trout, about 300 g (10 oz) each
salt and pepper
2 tablespoons lemon juice
lemon wedges and parsley sprigs, to garnish
orange and lollo biondo salad, to serve

Preheat grill. Shell hazelnuts, then spread in a single layer in grill pan and heat under grill, stirring frequently, until skins split. Tip nuts onto a tea towel and rub to remove skins. Chop nuts.

In a large frying pan, heat 55 g (2 oz/4 tablespoons) butter. Season trout inside and out with salt and pepper, then add 2 trout to the pan and fry for 12-15 minutes, turning once, until brown and cooked. Drain fish on absorbent kitchen paper, then transfer to a warm serving plate and keep warm while frying remaining fish in the same way.

Wipe pan with absorbent kitchen paper, add remaining butter, then fry chopped nuts until browned. Stir lemon juice into pan, then quickly pour mixture over fish. Garnish with lemon wedges and sprigs of parsley and serve with orange and lollo biondo salad.

Serves 4.

— TROUT WITH PARMA HAM —

4 trout, about 300 g (10 oz) each
pepper
1 lemon, quartered
4 sprigs basil or tarragon
4 slices Parma or prosciutto ham
lemon wedges and chervil sprigs, to garnish
tomato, lime, red chicory and asparagus salad, to serve

Preheat oven to 200C (400F/Gas 6). Season trout with pepper and a squeeze of lemon juice. Place a sprig of basil or tarragon inside each fish.

Wrap a slice of ham around each fish and season with pepper. Place fish in a large, shallow baking dish with loose ends of ham underneath.

Bake fish for 15-20 minutes until cooked through and flesh flakes. Garnish with lemon wedges and sprigs of chervil and serve with tomato, lime, red chicory and asparagus salad.

Serves 4.

TANDOORI TROUT

seeds from 6 cardamom pods
2 teaspoons cumin seeds
4 tablespoons plain yogurt, preferably Greek style
1 large clove garlic, chopped
2 tablespoons lime juice
2.5 cm (1 in) piece fresh ginger, chopped
1 teaspoon garam masala
pinch ground turmeric
¼ teaspoon cayenne pepper
salt
1 teaspoon red food colouring (optional)
2 trout, about 300 g (10 oz) each
oil for brushing
rice with chillies and tomato and onion salad
lemon and lime wedges and coriander sprigs, to garnish

Heat a small heavy pan, add cardamom and cumin seeds and heat until fragrant. Tip into a mortar or small bowl and crush with a pestle or end of a rolling pin. Put yogurt, garlic, lime juice, all the spices, cayenne pepper and salt into a blender and mix to a paste. Add food colouring, if using.

With the point of a sharp knife, make 3 deep slashes in each side of the trout. Spread spice mixture over trout, working it into the slashes. Place in a shallow, non-metallic dish, cover and leave to marinate in refrigerator for 4 hours. Preheat grill. Brush grill rack with oil. Sprinkle a little oil over fish and grill for about 7 minutes on each side. Serve with rice with chillies and tomato and onion salad, garnished with lemon and lime wedges and sprigs of coriander.

Serves 2.

TROUT & ARTICHOKE FRITTATA

1 medium or 2 small artichokes
45 g (1 ½ oz/3 tablespoons) unsalted butter
6 eggs
200 g (7 oz) cooked trout fillet, flaked
2 tablespoons chopped fresh parsley
salt and pepper
green salad, to serve
lemon wedges and parsley sprigs, to garnish

Snap off artichoke stems, then bend outer leaves backwards to remove them. Continue until pale inner cone is reached. Cut off tough top part of cone and remove hairy inner 'choke'. Trim artichoke, then quarter. Cut each quarter into 4 or 6 pieces.

In a 30 cm (12 in) frying pan, heat butter, add artichoke, saute for 2-3 minutes, then add a little water, cover and simmer until tender. Boil hard, uncovered, to evaporate off all water. Using a fork, lightly beat eggs with trout, chopped parsley, salt and pepper until yolks and whites are blended.

Pour eggs into pan and reduce heat to very low. Cook very gently for about 15 minutes until bulk is almost set and top is still creamy and moist. Meanwhile, preheat grill. Place pan under grill for 30-60 seconds until frittata is just set. Loosen edges with a spatula, then slide it onto a warm plate. Serve in wedges with a green salad, garnished with lemon wedges and sprigs of parsley.

Serves 4.

————— MIXED FISH POT —————

1 red mullet, red snapper, bream or trout,
   about 350 g (12 oz)
175 g (6 oz) piece sea bass
350 g (12 oz) monkfish fillet
½ bay leaf
1½ tablespoons olive oil
115 g (4 oz) fennel bulb
225 g (8 oz) small carrots
115 g (4 oz) onion, thinly sliced
1 small clove garlic, finely crushed
pinch saffron threads, toasted and crushed
150 ml (5 fl oz/⅔ cup) dry white wine
5 tablespoons single (light) cream
salt and pepper
½ bunch spring onions, cut diagonally into thin strips
dill sprigs, to garnish

Thickly slice mullet, snapper, bream or trout
and place head and tail in a small saucepan.
Remove skin and bones from bass and add
them to pan.

Trim fine skin from monkfish and add skin to
pan with bay leaf and 150 ml (5 fl oz/⅔ cup)
water. Simmer for 20 minutes then strain and
reserve the stock. Thickly slice raw bass and
monkfish.

In a flameproof casserole, heat oil. Cut fennel and carrots into thin strips and add to casserole with onion, garlic and saffron. Cook for 3-4 minutes. Add 4 tablespoons wine and boil until most of liquid has evaporated. Add remaining wine and boil until reduced by half.

Stir in reserved stock, 2½ tablespoons cream and monkfish and season with salt and pepper. Cover and cook very gently for 10 minutes.

Add mullet and bass, cover and cook for a further 10 minutes or until fish is just cooked. Gently stir in remaining cream and scatter spring onions over the top. Serve garnished with sprigs of dill.

Serves 4.

SALMON WITH AVOCADO SALSA

4 salmon fillets with skin, about 175 g (6 oz) each
2½ tablespoons olive oil
sea salt and pepper
lime wedges and coriander leaves, to garnish
SALSA:
1 ripe but firm avocado
2 large ripe tomatoes, peeled, seeded and finely chopped
½ small red onion, finely chopped
½-1 fresh red chilli, seeded and thinly sliced
1 clove garlic, finely chopped
2 tablespoons lime juice
2 tablespoons chopped fresh coriander
salt and pepper

To make salsa, halve avocado, discard stone, quarter each half and remove skin. Dice avocado flesh and mix with remaining salsa ingredients. Cover and chill in refrigerator for about 1 hour.

Dry fish well, then brush skin with some of olive oil. In a heavy frying pan, heat remaining oil until hot. Add salmon, skin side down, and cook for 10-15 minutes depending on thickness of fillets, until skin is quite crisp, sides are opaque and top is slightly soft as it should be 'rare'. Season salmon with sea salt and pepper, garnish with lime wedges and coriander leaves and serve with salsa.

Serves 4.

— SALMON WITH HERB SAUCE —

½ onion, chopped
1 carrot, chopped
1 stick celery, chopped
1 lemon, sliced
1.6 kg (3½ lb) salmon
bouquet garni of 2 bay leaves and sprig each rosemary,
    sage and parsley
175 ml (6 fl oz/¾ cup) dry white wine
salt and pepper
bunch watercress, roughly chopped
3 tablespoons chopped fresh parsley
2 tablespoons chopped fresh chervil
1 tablespoon chopped fresh dill
225 g (8 oz/1 cup) ricotta or low fat soft cheese
lime and lemon slices and herb sprigs, to garnish

Preheat oven to 220C (425F/Gas 7). Place a
large piece of foil on a large baking sheet.
Make a bed of vegetables and half the lemon
slices on the foil. Put salmon on vegetables
and add bouquet garni and remaining lemon
slices. Fold up foil, pour in wine, season with
pepper, then seal edges of foil tightly. Bake in
the oven for 1 hour. Remove baking sheet
from oven and leave fish to cool completely
in foil.

Strain cooking liquid, then boil it until
reduced to about 85 ml (3 fl oz/⅓ cup). Add
watercress and herbs and boil until softened.
Tip into a blender, add cheese and purée.
Season with salt and pepper, pour into a
serving bowl or jug and refrigerate. Lift fish
onto a rack. Carefully remove skin, fins and
fatty line that runs along spine. Transfer to a
large serving plate, garnish with lime and
lemon slices and sprigs of herbs and serve
with sauce.

Serves 6.

COULIBIAC

55 g (2 oz) long grain rice
salt and pepper
350 g (12 oz) spinach, stalks removed, torn
pinch freshly grated nutmeg
85 g (3 oz/6 tablespoons) butter
1 onion, finely chopped
200 ml (7 fl oz/scant 1 cup) milk
450 g (1 lb) salmon fillets
2 tablespoons plain flour
4 tablespoons sour cream
1½ tablespoons chopped fresh parsley
1½ tablespoons chopped fresh chives
2 hard-boiled eggs, coarsely chopped
4 large sheets filo pastry

In a saucepan, bring 150 ml (5 fl oz/⅔ cup) water to boil, add rice and salt, stir, then return to boil. Cover and cook for 12-15 minutes until rice is tender and water absorbed. Meanwhile, wash but do not dry spinach, put into a saucepan and heat until there is no visible liquid. Tip into a colander and press out surplus liquid. Season with salt, pepper and nutmeg. Leave to cool.

In a pan, heat 25 g (1 oz/2 tablespoons) butter, add onion and fry until softened but not coloured. Stir into rice with pepper. Cool. Pour milk into a shallow pan, add salmon, bring to boil, then poach for 10-15 minutes until only just cooked. Drain and reserve milk. Skin and flake fish.

Heat 25 g (1 oz/2 tablespoons) butter in a saucepan, stir in flour for 1 minute, then slowly pour in reserved milk, stirring. Bring to the boil, stirring, and simmer for about 4 minutes, stirring occasionally. Remove from heat, cool slightly then fold in salmon, cream, herbs, eggs and seasoning. Cool completely.

Preheat oven to 200C (400F/Gas 6). Butter a baking sheet. Melt remaining butter. Cut pastry in half. Lay one sheet on baking sheet, brush lightly with melted butter, then repeat with 3 more sheets pastry; keep remaining pastry covered with damp cloth.

Spoon rice onto pastry, leaving a 2.5 cm (1 in) border. Cover with spinach, then fish mixture. Lay a sheet of pastry over filling, brush with butter, then repeat with remaining pastry. Press edges together, then bake in the oven for about 25 minutes until pastry is crisp and golden.

Serves 4-6.

SALMON STIR-FRY

450 g (1 lb) medium slim asparagus, trimmed
2 tablespoons groundnut oil
300 g (10 oz) salmon, skinned, boned and cut into thin
    strips 2.5 cm (1 in) long
squeeze lemon juice
1 tablespoon light soy sauce
2 teaspoons sesame oil
salt and pepper
lightly toasted sesame seeds, to garnish
Chinese egg noodles, to serve

Slice asparagus diagonally into 1 cm (½ in) pieces. Bring a saucepan of salted water to boil, add asparagus and cook for 1½ minutes. Drain and rinse.

In a wok or large frying pan, heat groundnut oil, add asparagus and stir-fry for 1½ minutes.

Add salmon, lemon juice, soy sauce and sesame oil to pan and stir-fry for 2 minutes. Add black pepper and a little salt. Serve immediately sprinkled with sesame seeds, accompanied by Chinese egg noodles.

Serves 4.

CHINESE SALAD WITH SALMON

350 g (12 oz) Chinese noodles
1 tablespoon salted black beans, coarsely chopped
85 g (3 oz) beansprouts
1 tablespoon groundnut oil
450 g (1 lb) salmon fillets, cut into
   2.5 cm (1 in) cubes
2 teaspoons grated fresh ginger
2 tablespoons rice wine or medium sherry
2 teaspoons sesame oil
85 g (3 oz) watercress leaves and fine stalks
½ red pepper (capsicum), seeded and chopped

Cook noodles according to packet directions, drain and rinse well with cold water. Drain again, then put into a serving bowl, cover and refrigerate while preparing remaining ingredients. Soak black beans in 1-2 tablespoons hot water. Bring a pan of water to the boil, add beansprouts and boil for 1 minute. Drain, rinse under cold running water, then set aside. Heat groundnut oil in a frying pan, add salmon, in batches if necessary, and fry until just cooked and pale gold. Drain on absorbent kitchen paper.

Stir ginger, rice wine or sherry, sesame oil and half the watercress into pan. Boil for a few seconds, then add black beans and remove from heat. Add beansprouts, pepper (capsicum) and salmon to noodles, pour over warm dressing and garnish with remaining watercress.

Serves 4.

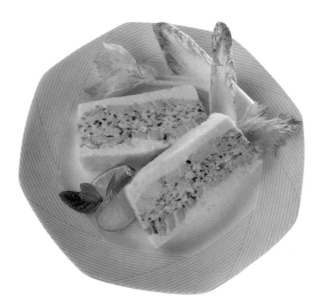

——— LAYERED FISH TERRINE ———

450 g (1 lb) salmon, skinned and boned
salt and white pepper
150 ml (5 fl oz/⅔ cup) medium-bodied dry white wine
2 small bunches watercress, trimmed
15 g (½ oz/1 tablespoon) butter
1 shallot, finely chopped
450 g (1 lb) firm white fish, such as hake, monkfish or
 cod, skinned, boned and cubed
2 egg whites
210 ml (7½ fl oz/scant 1 cup) double (heavy) cream,
 chilled
lime slices and mint sprigs, to garnish

Cut salmon into long strips, put in a dish, season lightly and pour the wine over it. Cover and leave for about 1 hour.

Meanwhile, boil a saucepan of lightly salted water, add watercress and blanch for 1 minute. Drain watercress, rinse under cold running water, drain again, then dry on absorbent kitchen paper; set aside.

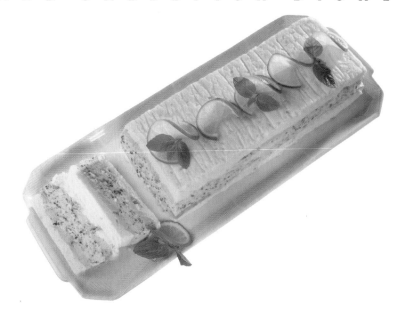

In a small saucepan, heat butter. Add shallot and cook gently until softened but not browned. Purée shallot with cubed white fish in a food processor. Add egg whites and season with salt and pepper. Mix for 1 minute, then slowly pour in cream. Remove and reserve two thirds of fish mixture. Add watercress to food processor and purée briefly. Chill both mixtures for 30 minutes.

Preheat oven to 180C (350F/Gas 4). Lightly oil a 25 × 9 cm (10 × 3½ in) terrine. Spread half the plain fish mixture in the terrine, then half the salmon strips followed by all the green mixture. Cover this with remaining salmon strips, then remaining white mixture.

Cover terrine with foil, place in a roasting tin and pour in enough boiling water to come halfway up sides of terrine. Bake in oven for about 40 minutes until a skewer inserted in centre comes out clean. Transfer terrine to a wire rack to cool, then refrigerate. Serve cut into slices, garnished with lime slices and sprigs of mint.

Serves 4-6.

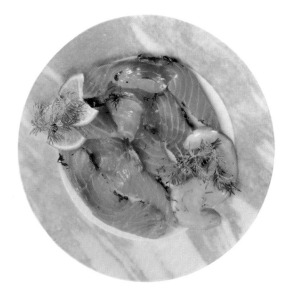

GRAVAD LAX

3 tablespoons sea salt
2-3 teaspoons light brown sugar
2 teaspoons crushed black peppercorns
6 tablespoons lime juice
large bunch dill
1.4-1.8 kg (3-4 lb) salmon, filleted, with skin
lime slices and dill sprigs, to garnish
DILL AND MUSTARD SAUCE:
3 tablespoons Dijon mustard
2 tablespoons white wine vinegar
1 tablespoon sugar
150 ml (5 fl oz/⅔ cup) grapeseed oil
2 tablespoons finely chopped fresh dill
salt and pepper

In a small bowl, mix together salt, sugar, peppercorns and lime juice. Spread some dill in a shallow non-metallic dish and add a quarter of salt mixture. Lay one salmon fillet, skin side down, in dish. Cover with plenty of dill and spoon over half remaining salt mixture. Place remaining salmon on top, skin-side uppermost. Cover salmon with remaining dill and pour over remaining salt mixture. Cover with greaseproof paper then plastic wrap.

Place a 900 g (2 lb) weight on top and leave in a cool place for 2 days, or bottom of refrigerator for 3 days, turning occasionally and spooning liquid back between fillets occasionally. To make sauce, mix together mustard, vinegar and sugar, then gradually whisk in oil. Add chopped dill and seasoning. Drain salmon well, pat dry and trim off any hard edges. Very thinly slice salmon on bias, discarding skin. Garnish with lime slices and sprigs of dill and serve with sauce.

Serves 8.

TUNA BASQUAISE

6 slices tuna, about 2.5cm (1 in) thick
4 cloves garlic
85 ml (3 fl oz/¹⁄₃ cup) olive oil
1 large onion, finely chopped
1 large red pepper (capsicum), seeded, cored and
   thinly sliced
1 green pepper (capsicum), seeded, cored and
   thinly sliced
400 g (14 oz) tomatoes, peeled, seeded and diced
1 tablespoon sun-dried tomato paste
3 sprigs thyme
1 bay leaf
salt and pepper
parsley sprigs, to garnish

Cut slits in tuna. Cut 2 cloves garlic into slivers and insert in slits in tuna. In a large frying pan, heat half the oil, add tuna and cook until lightly browned on both sides. Remove tuna from pan and set aside. Add remaining oil to pan, add onion and peppers (capsicums) and cook over moderate heat, stirring frequently, for about 10 minutes until soft.

Chop remaining garlic, add to pan, cook for 1 minute, then add tomatoes, tomato paste, thyme and bay leaf. Simmer, uncovered, for 15-20 minutes, stirring occasionally. Return tuna to pan, season with salt and pepper, then cover with buttered greaseproof paper and cook gently for 15 minutes. Serve garnished with sprigs of parsley.

Serves 6.

——— WARM TUNA NIÇOISE ———

700 g (1½ lb) small new potatoes
450 g (1 lb) green beans
2 tablespoons olive oil
4 tuna steaks, about 150 g (5 oz) each and 1 cm (½ in)
  thick
2 tomatoes, chopped
Niçoise or small black oil-cured olives, to garnish
DRESSING:
2 teaspoons wholegrain mustard
1 tablespoon anchovy paste
1 clove garlic, finely chopped
3 tablespoons red wine vinegar
4 tablespoons olive oil
2 teaspoons capers
pepper

To make dressing, whisk mustard, anchovy paste, garlic and vinegar together in a bowl or jug, then slowly pour in oil, whisking constantly. Whisk in capers and set aside.

Boil potatoes in their skins until tender, drain and then cut into 2 cm (¾ in) pieces and put into a bowl. Add pepper to dressing and lightly stir 3 tablespoons of dressing into potatoes.

Meanwhile, cut beans into 2.5 cm (1 in) lengths. Heat a large, heavy frying pan, add 1 tablespoon oil, then the beans (be careful they do not splatter). Stir-fry for about 5 minutes until tender but still crisp. Transfer beans to a bowl and stir in 1 tablespoon dressing.

Add remaining oil to pan. Season both sides of tuna with pepper, then add to pan and cook over a moderately high heat for about 4 minutes, turning once, until brown outside and still slightly rare in the middle.

Transfer tuna to a warm serving dish. Add tomatoes and trickle 1 tablespoon dressing over the top; trickle remainder over the tuna. Add beans and potatoes and scatter olives over them. Serve immediately.

Serves 4.

TUNA & GINGER VINAIGRETTE

2.5 cm (1 in) piece fresh ginger, finely chopped
2 large spring onions, white and some green parts,
   thinly sliced
225 ml (8 fl oz/1 cup) olive oil
juice 2 limes
2 tablespoons soy sauce
2 tablespoons sesame oil
1 bunch coriander, finely chopped
pepper
6 tuna steaks, about 150-175 g (5-6 oz) each
leek and red pepper (capsicum) stir-fry with
   sesame seeds
coriander sprigs, to garnish

Preheat grill. To make vinaigrette, stir together ginger, spring onions, olive oil, lime juice and soy sauce, then whisk in sesame oil. Add chopped coriander and season with pepper; set aside.

Grill tuna under a high heat for 3½-4 minutes each side, or a little longer for well-done fish. Spoon some dressing onto 6 plates and add the fish. Serve with leek and red pepper (capsicum) stir-fry, garnished with sprigs of coriander. Serve any remaining dressing separately.

Serves 6.

—— HERRINGS IN OATMEAL ——

about 1 tablespoon Dijon mustard
about 1½ teaspoons tarragon vinegar
85 ml (3 fl oz/⅓ cup) thick mayonnaise
85 ml (3 fl oz/⅓ cup) plain yogurt
4 herrings, about 225 g (8 oz) each, cleaned and heads
   and tails removed
salt and pepper
1 lemon, halved
115 g (4 oz) medium oatmeal
rice and artichoke heart salad, to serve
lemon wedges and coriander sprigs, to garnish

In a small bowl, beat mustard and vinegar to taste into mayonnaise and yogurt, then spoon into a small serving bowl and chill lightly.

Preheat grill. Place one fish on a board, cut-side down and opened out. Press gently along backbone with your thumbs. Turn fish over and carefully lift away backbone and attached bones.

Season with salt and pepper and squeeze lemon juice over both sides of fish, then fold in half, skin-side outwards. Repeat with remaining fish. Coat each fish evenly in oatmeal, pressing it in well but gently. Grill herrings for 3-4 minutes on each side until brown and crisp and flesh flakes easily. Serve hot with the mustard sauce, accompanied by a rice and artichoke heart salad and garnished with lemon wedges and sprigs of coriander.

Serves 4.

—MACKEREL WITH MUSTARD—

2 tablespoons Dijon mustard
4 tablespoons finely chopped fresh coriander
2 cloves garlic, finely crushed
2-3 teaspoons lemon juice
salt and pepper
4 mackerel, about 300 g (10 oz) each
rolled oats
tomato, fennel and thyme salad, to serve
lemon wedges and coriander sprigs, to garnish

Preheat grill. In a bowl, mix together mustard, coriander, garlic and lemon juice and season with salt and pepper.

Using the point of a sharp knife, cut 3 slashes on each side of the mackerel. Spoon mustard mixture into slashes and sprinkle with a few rolled oats. Wrap each fish in a large piece of foil and fold the edges of the foil together to seal tightly.

Place foil packages under hot grill for 5 minutes. Open foil, turn fish, reseal packages and cook for a further 2-3 minutes. Open foil, place fish under the grill and cook for 2-3 minutes until cooked. Serve with tomato, fennel and thyme salad, garnished with lemon wedges and sprigs of coriander.

Serves 4.

— MACKEREL WITH YOGURT —

½ cucumber, peeled
salt and pepper
175 ml (6 fl oz/¾ cup) thick plain yogurt, preferably
    Greek style
1¼ tablespoons chopped fresh mint
1 garlic clove, finely crushed
½ teaspoon harissa or pinch chilli powder
2 teaspoons ground cumin
2 tablespoons light olive oil
squeeze lemon juice
4 mackerel, cleaned
red chicory, bean and yellow pepper (capsicum) salad,
    to serve

Halve cucumber lengthways, scoop out seeds and thinly slice flesh.

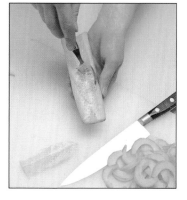

Spread flesh in a colander, sprinkle with salt and leave to drain for 30 minutes. Rinse cucumber, dry with absorbent kitchen paper, then mix with yogurt and mint. Cover and chill for 2 hours. Put garlic in a mortar, or small bowl, then pound in harissa or chilli powder, cumin and oil, using a pestle or end of a rolling pin. Add lemon juice and season with salt and pepper.

With the point of a sharp knife, cut 2 slashes in each side of the fish. Spread spice mixture over the fish and leave for 15-30 minutes. Preheat grill and cook fish for 7-8 minutes on each side. Serve with cucumber mixture, accompanied by red chicory, bean and yellow pepper (capsicum) salad.

Serves 4.

SARDINES IN CORIANDER SAUCE

1 kg (2 lb) sardines (at least 12)
4 tablespoons olive oil
grated rind 1½ limes
1½ tablespoons lime juice
¾ teaspoon finely crushed, toasted coriander seeds
3 tablespoons chopped fresh coriander
salt and pepper
coriander sprigs, to garnish
lime wedges, to serve

Put sardines in a shallow, non-metallic dish. Thoroughly whisk together oil, lime rind and juice, coriander seeds, chopped coriander and salt and pepper.

Pour coriander mixture over sardines and leave for 1 hour, turning sardines over once.

Preheat grill. Remove sardines from dish and grill for 4-5 minutes on each side, basting with coriander mixture. Serve sardines garnished with sprigs of coriander and accompanied by lime wedges.

Serves 4.

STUFFED SARDINES

12 sardines, cleaned
1 tablespoon each chopped fresh parsley, chives, dill,
    basil and 2 small sage leaves, chopped
1 clove garlic
25 g (1 oz) pine nuts, lightly toasted
pinch crushed dried chillies
2 tablespoons light virgin olive oil
salt and pepper
½ lemon
2½ tablespoons fresh breadcrumbs
grilled baby vegetables and lemon wedges, to serve

Preheat oven to 220C (425F/Gas 7). Oil a
wide, shallow baking dish. Cut heads and
tails from sardines.

Slit along underside of bodies to open them
out. Discard intestines. Wash cavities of fish,
then pat dry with absorbent kitchen paper.
Lay one fish, skin side uppermost, on a work
surface then, using your thumbs, press gently
along centre of the back to dislodge backbone. Turn fish over and gently pull away
backbone. Repeat with remaining sardines.

Finely chop herbs, garlic and nuts, then mix
with crushed chillies, 1 tablespoon oil and
salt and pepper. Lay 6 sardines, skin side
down, in a single layer in dish. Squeeze over
some lemon juice, then spread some herb
mixture on each fish. Cover with remaining
sardines, skin side up. Sprinkle with breadcrumbs, then trickle remaining oil over the
top. Bake for about 10 minutes until golden.
Serve hot or at room temperature with baby
vegetables and lemon wedges.

Serves 4.

—JOHN DORY WITH ORANGE—

4 John Dory fillets, about 165 g (5½ oz) each
4 sprigs mint
4 tablespoons dry white vermouth
finely grated rind and juice 1 orange
1-2 tablespoons virgin olive oil
salt and pepper
orange slices, to garnish

Preheat oven to 180C (350F/Gas 4). Cut 4 pieces foil each large enough to enclose one piece of fish. Oil top side of each piece. Place a fish in centre of each piece of foil.

Pinch out centre of each mint sprig and reserve for garnish. Finely chop remaining mint, then mix with vermouth, orange rind and juice, olive oil and salt and pepper.

Fold up sides of foil, spoon one quarter of orange mixture over each fish, then seal edges of foil tightly. Place foil parcels on a baking sheet and bake for 12-15 minutes. Serve garnished with orange slices and reserved mint sprigs.

Serves 4.

— FISH & WATERCRESS SAUCE —

4 John Dory, brill or porgy fillets, about 175 g (6 oz)
  each, skinned
mixed salad, to serve
SAUCE:
25 g (1 oz/2 tablespoons) unsalted butter
leaves and fine stems of 1 large bunch watercress
150 ml (5 fl oz/²⁄₃ cup) mayonnaise
about 1 tablespoon lemon juice
salt and pepper

Bring base of steamer filled with water to the
boil. Lay fish fillets in a steaming basket,
cover basket, then place over steamer base
and steam for about 5 minutes.

Meanwhile, to make sauce, in a saucepan,
heat butter, add watercress and sauté for 2-3
minutes.

Transfer watercress and butter to a blender,
add mayonnaise and mix briefly then, with
motor running, slowly trickle in 1 tablespoon
lemon juice. Season with salt and pepper and
add extra lemon juice if necessary. Season
fish and serve with mixed salad, accompanied
by watercress sauce.

Serves 4.

BREAM DUGLÉRÉ

4 bream fillets, about 175 g (6 oz) each
salt and pepper
250 ml (9 fl oz/generous 1 cup) fish stock
6 tablespoons medium-bodied dry white wine
150 ml (5 fl oz/⅔ cup) double (heavy) cream
1 large sun-ripened beefsteak tomato, peeled, seeded
　and cut into 1 cm (½ in) strips
basil or parsley sprigs, to garnish

Season fish, then place in a single layer in a well buttered frying pan. Add stock and wine and bring just to the boil. Reduce heat, cover pan and poach fish for 4-6 minutes.

Using a fish slice, transfer fish to a warm plate, cover and keep warm. Boil cooking liquid rapidly until reduced to a quarter. Stir cream into pan and simmer for 2-3 minutes.

Add tomato strips and heat gently for 1 minute. Season sauce, then pour it over the fish. Serve garnished with basil or parsley sprigs.

Serves 4.

— BAKED BREAM WITH FENNEL —

2 fennel bulbs, thinly sliced
1 red onion, thinly sliced
3 cloves garlic, sliced
1 lemon, peeled and thinly sliced
3 small sprigs rosemary
2 sea bream, about 575 g (1¼ lb) each, cleaned
    and scaled
1 tablespoon fennel seeds, cracked
salt and pepper
5 tablespoons olive oil
rosemary sprigs, to garnish

Preheat oven to 180C (350F/Gas 4). Spread fennel, onion, garlic, lemon and rosemary in a baking dish large enough to hold fish.

Cook in oven for about 8 minutes. Meanwhile, with the point of a sharp knife, cut 2 slashes in each side of the fish and put half the fennel seeds inside each fish.

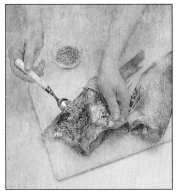

Place fish on vegetables, season with salt and pepper and pour oil over them. Bake for 20-25 minutes, turning fish halfway through, until vegetables and fish are tender. Serve garnished with rosemary sprigs.

Serves 4-6.

– BREAM WITH LEMON & HERBS –

2 tablespoons chopped fresh mixed herbs, such as
   thyme, rosemary, marjoram, fennel and basil
½ clove garlic, chopped
juice ½ lemon
salt and pepper
3 tablespoons extra virgin olive oil
4 bream fillets, about 250 g (9 oz) each
finely grated lemon rind and slices and parsley sprigs,
   to garnish

Preheat oven to 200C (400F/Gas 6). Briefly
chop together herbs and garlic. Put into a
bowl, stir in lemon juice, season with salt and
pepper, then gradually beat in oil using a fork
so mixture thickens; set aside.

Cut 4 pieces of greaseproof paper each large
enough to enclose a fish. Place one fish on
each piece of paper and spoon over herb
mixture. Fold paper loosely over fish and seal
edges tightly.

Place parcels on a baking sheet and cook in
oven for about 15 minutes. Serve fish in the
paper parcels, garnished with lemon rind and
slices and parsley sprigs.

Serves 4.

CHINESE-STYLE BREAM

4 tablespoons soy sauce
1 carrot, cut into fine strips
3 spring onions, cut into fine strips
2.5 cm (1 in) piece fresh ginger, finely shredded
575 g (1¼ lb) bream fillets
2 tablespoons sesame oil
2 tablespoons groundnut oil
1 fresh red chilli, cut into rings, seeded
1 clove garlic, shredded
chopped fresh chives, to garnish

Put a little of the soy sauce on a large serving plate.

Mix together carrot, spring onions and ginger and use half to make a bed on the plate for the fish. Place fish on vegetables. Scatter over remaining vegetables, then trickle over remaining soy sauce. Place plate in steaming basket and cover basket. Fill bottom of steamer with water and bring to the boil. Put basket on steamer and cook for 10-14 minutes.

Meanwhile, in a small saucepan, very gently heat sesame and groundnut oils. Add chilli and garlic and cook for 5-7 minutes. Remove plate from steaming basket, baste fish with cooking juices, then pour over hot oil, garlic and chilli. Serve garnished with chopped chives.

Serves 2.

FISH PLAKI

about 1.15 kg (2½ lb) fish, such as bream, bass, grey
   mullet, red snapper or pompano, scaled
juice ½ lemon
2 tablespoons olive oil
1 onion, chopped
1 carrot, finely chopped
1 stick celery, chopped
2 cloves garlic, chopped
1 teaspoon coriander seeds, crushed
450 g (1 lb) tomatoes, peeled, seeded and chopped
3 halves sun-dried tomato, finely chopped
85 ml (3 fl oz/⅓ cup) dry white wine
leaves from bunch parsley, finely chopped
salt and pepper
parsley sprigs, to garnish

Preheat oven to 190C (375F/Gas 5). Put fish
into a baking dish and squeeze over lemon
juice. Heat oil in a saucepan, add onion,
carrot and celery and cook, stirring occasionally, until onion has softened but not
coloured. Stir in garlic and cook for about 3
minutes. Stir coriander seeds, tomatoes, sun-
dried tomatoes, wine and parsley into pan,
season with salt and pepper and simmer for a
few minutes until well blended.

Using a fish slice, lift fish and pour about a
quarter of the tomato mixture underneath.
Lay fish down again and pour over remaining
tomato mixture. Cover dish and bake in the
oven for about 40 minutes. Serve garnished
with parsley sprigs.

Serves 4.

-SKATE WITH ANCHOVY SAUCE-

4 small skate wings
1 tablespoon olive oil
15 g (½ oz/1 tablespoon) unsalted butter
salt and pepper
sugar snap peas and new potatoes, to serve
basil sprigs, to garnish
SAUCE:
1 large clove garlic
6 anchovy fillets, chopped
2½ tablespoons capers
2½ teaspoons wholegrain mustard
1½ tablespoons chopped fresh basil
3 tablespoons chopped fresh parsley
6 teaspoons lime juice
3 tablespoons virgin olive oil
black pepper

To make sauce, crush garlic with anchovies in a small bowl. Mix in capers, mustard, basil, parsley and lime juice, then gradually whisk in oil. Season with black pepper and set aside.

Season skate wings. In a large non-stick frying pan, heat oil and butter. Add 2 skate wings and fry for about 4 minutes on each side until lightly browned. Transfer skate to absorbent kitchen paper and fry remaining skate in same way. Return skate to pan, pour in sauce and heat briefly until warmed through. Serve with sugar snap peas and new potatoes, garnished with sprigs of basil.

Serves 4.

STIR-FRIED SQUID

1 kg (2 lb) small squid
1½ tablespoons groundnut oil
2 cloves garlic, slivered
1 cm (½ in) piece ginger, finely chopped
2 plump stalks lemon grass, finely crushed and chopped
4 spring onions, white and some green part, sliced
1 tablespoon rice wine or medium dry sherry
1 tablespoon chopped fresh parsley and basil
parsley sprigs and lemon wedges, to garnish

Hold head of each squid in turn just below the eyes and gently pull from body pouch; the soft innards including ink sac will come with it. Discard innards.

Pull back rim of body pouch to locate fine quill-shaped pen. Carefully pull out and discard pen. Cut head fom tentacles just below eyes; discard head. Chop tentacles. Cut out small round of cartilage at base of tentacles. Squeeze beak-like mouth in centre of tentacles to remove. Slip your fingers under skin of body pouch, peel off then cut edible fins from body. Rinse squid under cold running water and dry well. Thinly slice squid.

In a wok or large frying pan, heat oil. Add garlic, ginger and lemon grass and cook gently for 1 minute. Increase heat, add squid and stir fry for 1 minute. Lower heat, add spring onions and cook for a further minute. Add wine, heat briefly, then sprinkle with chopped parsley and basil. Garnish with parsley sprigs and lemon wedges.

Serves 4.

STUFFED SQUID

about 12 small squid
4 tablespoons olive oil
1 small onion, finely chopped
2 cloves garlic, chopped
4 spring onions, chopped
4 anchovy fillets, chopped
6 tomatoes, peeled, seeded and chopped
2 tablespoons chopped mixed herbs
2 tablespoons fresh breadcrumbs
2 egg yolks
salt and pepper
1 lemon, halved
lemon and cucumber slices and chervil sprigs,
   to garnish

Prepare squid as for Stir-Fried Squid
(opposite) but do not slice bodies. In a frying
pan, heat 1 tablespoon oil, add onion, garlic,
spring onions and squid tentacles and cook
until onions are tender. Stir in anchovies,
tomatoes, herbs and breadcrumbs and cook,
stirring, for 1 minute, then remove from heat
and stir in egg yolks. Season with plenty of
pepper.

Preheat oven to 180C (350F/Gas 4). Oil a
shallow baking dish. Divide herb mixture
between squid bodies, taking care not to
overfill them. Close opening with wooden
cocktail sticks. Place squid in a single layer in
baking dish, squeeze lemon juice over them,
sprinkle with remaining oil and season. Bake
in the oven for about 20 minutes until tender,
basting with cooking juices occasionally.
Serve garnished with lemon and cucumber
slices and chervil sprigs.

Serves 4.

– TURKISH SWORDFISH KEBABS –

575 g (1¼ lb) swordfish, cut into cubes measuring
 about 2.5 × 4 cm (1 × 1½ in)
pasta, to serve
lime wedges and parsley sprigs, to garnish
MARINADE:
4 tablespoons lemon juice
4 tablespoons olive oil
1 shallot, finely chopped
3 fresh bay leaves, torn
1½ teaspoons paprika
salt and pepper
LEMON SAUCE:
3 tablespoons olive oil
3 tablespoons lemon juice
3 tablespoons chopped fresh parsley

To prepare marinade, mix the ingredients
together. Lay swordfish in a single layer in a
wide, shallow, non-metallic dish. Pour over
marinade, turn fish so it is evenly coated,
then cover and leave in a cool place for 4-5
hours, turning fish occasionally.

Mix together the sauce ingredients and
season with salt and pepper; set aside.
Preheat a grill or barbecue. Oil a grill rack.
Remove fish from marinade and thread onto
4 skewers. Grill or barbecue fish for 4-5
minutes each side, basting frequently. Serve
with the sauce on a bed of pasta, garnished
with lime wedges and sprigs of parsley.

Serves 4.

– SWORDFISH WITH TOMATOES –

3 tablespoons olive oil
4 swordfish steaks
1 small onion, finely chopped
2 cloves garlic, crushed
575 g (1¼ lb) tomatoes, skinned, seeded and chopped
2 halves sun-dried tomatoes, finely chopped
2 tablespoons chopped fresh parsley
1 bay leaf, torn
pepper
8 oil-cured black olives, halved and stoned
rice and courgette (zucchini) batons, to serve
basil sprigs, to garnish

In a frying pan, heat half the oil. Add fish and cook quickly to brown on both sides.

Transfer fish to a plate. Heat remaining oil in pan, add onion and garlic and cook until softened but not coloured. Stir in chopped tomatoes, sun-dried tomatoes, chopped parsley and bay leaf, stir for about 1 minute, then boil until thickened.

Season tomato mixture with pepper, add fish and baste with sauce. Cook gently, turning fish once, for 10-15 minutes until fish is cooked through. Just before the end of the cooking time, scatter stoned olives over the top. Serve with rice and courgette (zucchini) batons, garnished with sprigs of basil.

Serves 4.

ESCABECHE

6-8 red snapper, red sea bream or catfish fillets, cleaned
   and scaled
3 tablespoons seasoned flour
3 tablespoons olive oil
2-3 tablespoons chopped fresh coriander
MARINADE:
large pinch saffron threads, toasted
2 tablespoons olive oil
2 red onions, thinly sliced
2 red peppers (capsicums), seeded and sliced
½ teaspoon dried chilli flakes
1 ½ teaspoons cumin seeds, lightly crushed
finely grated rind and juice 1 orange
2-3 tablespoons rice vinegar
pinch caster sugar
salt and pepper

To make marinade, crush saffron, then soak
in warm water for 10 minutes. In a frying pan,
heat oil and gently cook onions for 2 minutes.
Add peppers (capsicums), chilli flakes and
cumin and fry until vegetables are soft. Stir in
saffron and liquid, orange rind and juice,
vinegar, sugar and salt and pepper. Bubble for
a few minutes, then leave to cool.

Toss fish in flour. In a frying pan, heat the 3
tablespoons oil, add fish and fry for 2-3
minutes on each side until just cooked and
browned. Place the fish in a single layer
in a shallow, non-metallic dish and pour
marinade over it. Cover and refrigerate for
4-12 hours. Return to room temperature 15
minutes before serving. Stir in coriander.

Serves 6-8 as first course.

Note: Garnish with orange slices and sprigs
of coriander, if wished.

—CAJUN-STYLE RED SNAPPER—

2 red snapper, about 575-700 g (1¼-1½ lb) each
25 g (1 oz/2 tablespoons) unsalted butter
2 tablespoons olive oil
SPICE MIX:
1 plump clove garlic
½ onion
1 teaspoon salt
1 teaspoon paprika
½ teaspoon cayenne pepper
½ teaspoon ground cumin
½ teaspoon mustard powder
1 teaspoon each dried thyme and dried oregano
½ teaspoon pepper

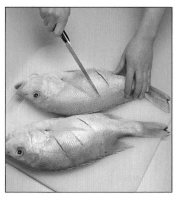

With the point of a sharp knife, cut 3 slashes on each side of both fish.

To make spice mix, crush together garlic and onion with salt in a pestle and mortar or in a bowl using the end of a rolling pin. Stir in remaining spice mix ingredients. Spread some spice mix over each fish, making sure it goes into the slashes. Lay the fish in a shallow dish, cover and leave in a cool place for 1 hour.

In a large frying pan, heat butter and oil until sizzling. Add fish and fry for about 4 minutes on each side until fish is cooked and spice coating has blackened.

Serves 2.

Note: Serve with a colourful selection of tomato, lemon and lime slices with thyme and parsley sprigs.

– RED SNAPPER & MUSHROOMS –

175 g (6 oz) mushrooms, sliced
4 spring onions, green and white parts, finely chopped
two 700 g (1½ lb) red snapper or 1.5 kg (3 lb) grouper,
    cleaned and scaled but with head and tail left on
2½ tablespoons chopped fresh coriander
1 tablespoon olive oil
1 tablespoon melted butter
2 tablespoons lemon juice
300 ml (10 fl oz/1¼ cups) medium-bodied dry
    white wine
150 ml (5 fl oz/⅔ cup) freshly squeezed tangerine juice
salt and pepper
tangerine wedges, to garnish

Preheat oven to 200C (400F/Gas 6). Butter a baking dish just large enough to hold the fish. Scatter mushrooms and spring onions in bottom of dish, then place fish on top.

Sprinkle chopped coriander over fish. Mix together oil, butter, lemon juice, wine and tangerine juice and season with salt and pepper. Pour mixture over fish. Bake in the oven for 20-30 minutes until flesh flakes. If cooking juices are too thin, transfer fish and mushrooms to a warm serving plate and keep warm. Pour juices into a pan and boil to concentrate slightly, then pour them over fish. Serve garnished with tangerine wedges.

Serves 4.

—SWORDFISH WITH SAUCE—

3½ tablespoons olive oil
1 clove garlic, finely chopped
300 g (10 oz) courgettes (zucchini), diced
2 tablespoons fish stock or dry white wine
2 swordfish steaks, halved, or 4 mahi mahi
  (dolphinfish) fillets
10 basil leaves
1 large tomato, peeled, seeded and chopped
salt and pepper
rice, to serve
basil sprigs, to garnish

In a frying pan, heat 1½ tablespoons olive oil, add garlic and cook gently until golden. Add courgettes (zucchini) and stock or wine.

Place fish on courgettes (zucchini) and put basil leaves and tomato on top of fish. Cover pan tightly and cook gently for about 10 minutes. Transfer fish, with tomato, to warm plates. Season with salt and pepper, cover and keep warm. If necessary, continue to cook courgettes (zucchini) until tender.

Purée courgettes (zucchini), basil and garlic in a blender and slowly pour in 1-2 tablespoons oil and sufficient cooking water to make a soft purée. Season. Add courgette (zucchini) purée to plate with the fish. Serve with rice, garnished with sprigs of basil.

Serves 4.

CANTONESE PRAWNS

1 orange
2 tablespoons soy sauce
2 tablespoons clear honey
2 tablespoons dry sherry
2 tablespoons white wine vinegar
1 teaspoon five spice powder
700 g (1½ lb) raw jumbo (king) prawns, peeled and
    dark vein removed
spring onions, to garnish

With a vegetable peeler or small sharp knife, remove 6 strips of zest from orange, taking care not to include any white pith.

Cut strips into fine shreds, add to a small saucepan of boiling water and blanch for 2 minutes. Drain then put into the empty pan with soy sauce, honey, sherry, vinegar and five spice powder. Squeeze juice from orange and add to pan. Simmer for 3-4 minutes, then allow to cool.

Place prawns in a shallow dish, pour over soy mixture and leave to stand for 1 hour. In a frying pan, stir-fry prawns in the sauce for 2-4 minutes until prawns are pink and fully cooked. Serve garnished with spring onions.

Serves 4-6.

Variation: Use pomfret or pompano instead of prawns.

— PRAWNS WITH ASIAN SAUCE —

700 g (1½ lb) raw jumbo (king) prawns
lime wedges and basil sprigs, to garnish
MARINADE:
handful Thai or ordinary fresh basil, finely chopped
2 tablespoons finely chopped garlic
2 tablespoons finely chopped fresh ginger
2 tablespoons finely chopped green chillies
2 teaspoons rice wine or medium dry sherry
2½ tablespoons groundnut oil
1 teaspoon Chinese sesame oil
salt and pepper

To make marinade, pound ingredients together in a pestle and mortar or using the end of a rolling pin in a bowl.

Discard legs and heads from prawns then, using strong scissors, cut prawns lengthways in half leaving tail end intact. Remove dark intestinal vein. Rub marinade over prawns, spoon any remaining marinade over them, cover and leave in a cool place for 1 hour.

Preheat grill or barbecue. Cook prawns in a single layer for about 3 minutes until curled, or 'butterflied', and bright pink. Garnish with lime wedges and sprigs of basil. Serve any remaining marinade separately.

Serves 4-6.

BAKED PRAWNS & COURGETTES

3 courgettes (zucchini), thinly sliced lengthways
55 g (2 oz/1 cup) crumbled bread, crusts removed
small handful parsley, thyme, oregano and mint,
    chopped together
2½ tablespoons freshly grated Parmesan cheese
pinch chilli powder
salt
12 raw jumbo (king) prawns, peeled and dark
    vein removed
3-4 tablespoons olive oil
lemon and lime wedges and oregano sprigs, to garnish

Preheat oven to 200C (400F/Gas 6). Oil 4
large, individual heatproof dishes. Steam
courgette (zucchini) slices for 2 minutes.

Mix together bread, herbs, cheese, chilli
powder and a little salt. Place a layer of
courgette (zucchini) slices on bottom of each
dish and sprinkle with half the bread mixture.
Arrange 3 prawns in each dish, scatter over
some of the bread mixture and moisten with a
little oil.

Cover with courgette (zucchini) slices, then
remaining bread mixture. Trickle over a little
oil, then cover dishes tightly with foil. Pierce
a few holes with a cocktail stick. Bake in the
oven for 5-7 minutes. Serve garnished with
lemon and lime wedges and sprigs of oregano.

Serves 4.

——— INDIAN-STYLE PRAWNS ———

1½ tablespoons oil
1 large onion, sliced
2 cloves garlic, crushed
1-2 green chillies, seeded and finely chopped
1 green pepper (capsicum), seeded and finely chopped
1 cm (½ in) piece fresh ginger, grated
1¼ teaspoons each cumin and coriander seeds, toasted
    and crushed
1 teaspoon ground cinnamon
pinch saffron threads, toasted and crushed
salt
700 g (1½ lb) raw medium or large prawns, peeled
115 ml (4 fl oz) plain yogurt, preferably strained
    Greek style
rice, to serve
mint leaves and yogurt, to garnish

In a non-stick pan, heat oil. Add onion, garlic, chilli and pepper (capsicum) and cook fairly gently until softened and lightly browned. Stir in ginger, cumin, coriander and cinnamon and cook over a slightly higher heat for 1-2 minutes. Add saffron and salt, cover with water, then simmer uncovered for 20 minutes, stirring occasionally. Add prawns and more water, if necessary, to come halfway up prawns. Cook gently for about 4 minutes until prawns turn pink.

Transfer prawns to a warm plate. Boil cooking juices hard until they are syrupy. Stir a little of the juice into the yogurt, then stir back into pan. Heat through, stirring, but do not allow to boil. Add prawns and turn them in the sauce. Serve with rice, garnished with mint and a swirl of yogurt.

Serves 4.

SHRIMP RISOTTO

575 g (1¼ lb) cooked shrimps or small prawns
   with shells
bouquet garni
5 black peppercorns
1 clove garlic, crushed
½ onion stuck with 1 clove
300 ml (10 fl oz/1¼ cups) medium-bodied dry
   white wine
2 shallots, finely chopped
65 g (2½ oz/5 tablespoons) unsalted butter
pinch saffron threads, toasted and crushed
300 g (10 oz) arborio (Italian risotto) rice
2 tablespoons chopped fresh tarragon
salt and pepper

Peel shrimps and set aside.

Put shrimp shells, bouquet garni, peppercorns, garlic, onion, wine and 1 litre (35 fl oz/
scant 4½ cups) water in a saucepan, bring to
the boil and simmer for 20 minutes. Strain
through a sieve, pressing hard on shells.
Measure 1.25 litres (40 fl oz/5 cups) stock;
make up with water if necessary. Bring to the
boil.

In a thick-bottomed saucepan, cook shallots
in half the butter until translucent. Stir in
saffron and rice, using a wooden spoon, and
cook, stirring, for 1-2 minutes until rice is
well coated and has absorbed the butter.

Over a moderate heat, stir in about 150 ml (5 fl oz/⅔ cup) boiling stock, and continue to cook at a steady, but not too violent, bubble, stirring constantly, until there is no liquid and rice is creamy. Stir in a further 150 ml (5 fl oz/⅔ cup) boiling stock.

Continue to cook risotto, gradually adding smaller amounts of stock until rice is soft outside but is firm within, creamy and bound together, neither moist nor dry; about 15-20 minutes altogether. Add shrimps towards end of cooking time.

Remove pan from the heat, dice remaining butter and stir in with the tarragon. Cover and leave for 1 minute for the butter to be absorbed. Stir, taste and add salt, if necessary, then serve immediately.

Serves 4.

Note: Garnish with sprigs of tarragon, if wished.

SCALLOP, PRAWN & MINT SALAD

115 ml (4 fl oz/½ cup) dry white wine
½ onion, chopped
1 bay leaf
4 black peppercorns, crushed
450 g (1 lb) small courgettes (zucchini)
450 g (1 lb) shelled scallops
450 g (1 lb) raw large prawns, peeled
2 tomatoes, peeled, seeded and chopped
about 18 small mint leaves
DRESSING:
3-4 tablespoons lime juice
½ teaspoon finely grated lime rind
½ clove garlic, finely chopped
115 ml (4 fl oz/½ cup) extra virgin olive oil
2 tablespoons chopped fresh parsley
salt and pepper

Heat wine, onion, bay leaf and peppercorns with 550 ml (18 fl oz/2¼ cups) water in a saucepan, simmer for 15 minutes, then add courgettes (zucchini) and cook for about 8 minutes until tender but crisp. Remove courgettes (zucchini) and drain on absorbent kitchen paper. Add scallops and prawns to pan and poach until scallops just turn opaque, about 2 minutes, and prawns become pink, 3-4 minutes.

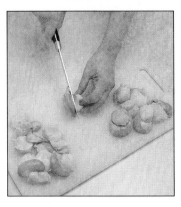

Drain seafood and cool under cold running water. Halve scallops horizontally. Cut courgettes (zucchini) into thin strips. Put into a serving dish with seafood, tomatoes and mint. To make dressing, whisk ingredients together, pour over salad and toss gently. Cover and chill for 30 minutes.

Serves 6.

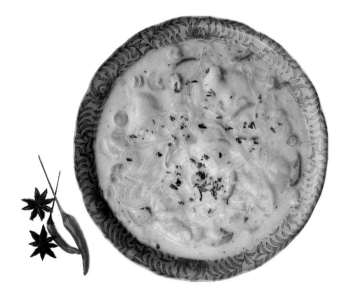

– THAI PRAWN & NOODLE SOUP –

425 ml (15 fl oz/scant 2 cups) fish stock
2 stalks lemon grass, crushed and chopped
2 small star anise pods
2 cloves garlic, chopped
425 ml (15 fl oz/scant 2 cups) coconut milk
8 large raw prawns, shelled
4 shelled scallops, halved horizontally
85 g (3 oz) clear vermicelli, soaked in cold water for
    10 minutes then drained
2 spring onions, thinly sliced
2 fresh red chillies, seeded and sliced
juice 1½ limes
1 tablespoon fish sauce
1 tablespoon chopped fresh coriander

Bring stock to the boil in a saucepan, add lemon grass, star anise and garlic, then simmer, uncovered, for 5 minutes. Cover and leave to stand for 30 minutes.

Add coconut milk to pan and heat to simmering point. Add prawns and scallops, poach for 1 minute, then add noodles, spring onions and chillies and cook for a further minute until prawns are pink. Remove pan from heat and stir in lime juice, fish sauce and chopped coriander.

Serves 4.

— MEDITERRANEAN FISH SOUP —

1.15 kg (2½ lb) mixed fish and shellfish, such as
   monkfish, red mullet, bass, bream, snapper, prawns,
   mussels, cleaned
pinch saffron threads, toasted and crushed
5 tablespoons olive oil
2 Spanish onions, sliced
1 stick celery, sliced
3 cloves garlic, chopped
3 large tomatoes, peeled
bouquet garni of 1 bay leaf, sprig each dried thyme and
   fennel, 3 parsley sprigs and a strip dried orange peel
1.2 litres (2¼ pints/5½ cups) fish stock
salt and pepper
torn basil or chopped fresh parsley, to garnish
French bread, to serve

Skin and fillet fish (see page 10) and cut into
fairly large pieces. Remove shellfish from
their shells. Soak saffron in 2 tablespoons
warm water for 10 minutes. In a large saucepan, heat oil. Add onions, celery and garlic
and cook gently until softened. Chop
tomatoes and add to pan with bouquet garni.
Arrange fish on vegetables, add saffron
liquid, then pour in sufficient stock to cover
fish. Simmer, uncovered, for 6 minutes.

Add shellfish and mussels to pan and cook for
a further 3-4 minutes until shellfish are just
tender and mussels open; discard any mussels
that remain closed. Season with salt and
pepper. Serve garnished with basil or parsley
and accompanied by French bread.

Serves 6.

SEAFOOD GUMBO

2 tablespoons olive oil
2 onions, chopped, and 2 cloves garlic, crushed
1 green pepper (capsicum), seeded and chopped
1 stick celery, chopped
2 tablespoons seasoned flour
685 ml (24 fl oz/3 cups) fish stock
400 g (14 oz) can chopped tomatoes
85 g (3 oz) cooked ham, chopped
bouquet garni
225 g (8 oz) fresh okra, sliced
225 g (8 oz) each white crabmeat and cooked
    peeled prawns
400 g (14 oz) redfish fillets or other firm white fish
    fillets, cut into chunks
lemon juice and dash Tabasco sauce
450 g (1 lb) boiled long-grain rice, to serve

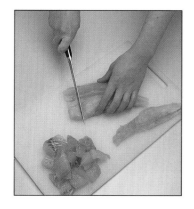

In a heavy flameproof casserole, heat oil.
Add onions and cook until softened. Add
garlic, pepper (capsicum) and celery and
cook, stirring frequently, for 5 minutes.
Sprinkle over flour and stir for 1 minute. Stir
stock, tomatoes, ham and bouquet garni into
casserole, partially cover and simmer for 30
minutes. Add okra and simmer, covered, for
30 minutes.

Chop crabmeat and set aside. Add fish to
casserole and cook for about 7 minutes. Add
crabmeat and prawns and cook for about 2½
minutes until prawns are hot. Add lemon
juice and Tabasco sauce to taste. Spoon rice
into warm serving bowls and ladle gumbo
over it.

Serves 4-6.

Note: Sprinkle chopped fresh parsley over
the top, if wished.

LOBSTER WITH BASIL DRESSING

4 lobsters, about 450-575 g (1-1¼ lb) each, cooked
   (see Note)
lamb's lettuce salad and lemon wedges, to serve
DRESSING:
55 g (2 oz) sun-dried tomatoes in olive oil, drained
   and chopped
1 small bunch basil, chopped
4 tablespoons walnut oil
2 tablespoons Spanish sherry vinegar
pepper

To make dressing, chop tomatoes and basil
together. Whisk together oil and vinegar,
then stir in tomatoes and basil. Season with
black pepper.

Using a large heavy knife and working from
head to tail along the back, split lobsters in
half. Remove and discard intestine that runs
through centre to tail, the stomach from near
the head, and the spongy gills.

Brush cut side of lobsters generously with
dressing and set aside for 15 minutes. Preheat
grill. Grill lobster for about 3 minutes. Meanwhile, gently warm remaining dressing in a
small saucepan. Brush lobster with dressing
and serve with lamb's lettuce salad and lemon
wedges. Serve remaining dressing separately.

Serves 4.

Note: If possible, order the lobsters from your
fishmonger and ask for them to be only three
quarters cooked. Use them the same day.

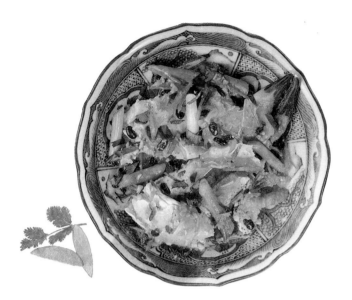

— CRAB & BLACK BEAN SAUCE —

700 g (1½ lb) fresh whole crab, cooked (see Note)
1¼ tablespoons groundnut oil
2-3 cloves garlic, crushed
3 whole spring onions, cut into 5 cm (2 in) pieces
three 0.5 cm (¼ in) slices fresh ginger, chopped
2 tablespoons fermented black beans
2 fresh red chillies, seeded and thinly sliced
1¼ tablespoons light soy sauce
2 tablespoons rice wine or medium sherry
115 ml (4 fl oz/½ cup) fish stock, preferably made
   from prawn shells and heads
coriander sprigs, to garnish

Detach claws and legs from crab and divide claws at joints. Using nutcrackers or a sharp heavy knife, lightly crack claws and legs so as not to damage the flesh within. Place crab on its back with tail flap towards you. Holding shell, press body section upwards from under tail flap and ease out with thumbs. Pull off inedible grey gills and discard. Using the knife, cut crab body into quarters. Using a spoon, remove stomach bag and mouth from back shell. Scrape out brown meat. Heat a wok or large frying pan, then add oil.

When it is hot, add garlic, spring onions and ginger and stir-fry until fragrant. Add black beans, chillies and crab, stir-fry for 2 minutes, then add soy sauce, rice wine and stock. Tip contents of wok or frying pan into a flameproof casserole. Cover and cook for 5 minutes. Serve garnished with coriander.

Serves 4.

Note: If possible, order a crab from your fishmongers and ask for it to be only three quarters cooked. Use it the same day.

CRAB SOUFFLÉ

45 g (1½ oz/3 tablespoons) butter
1 tablespoon grated onion
45 g (1½ oz/5 tablespoons) plain flour
175 ml (6 fl oz/¾ cup) milk
150 g (5 oz/⅔ cup) soft cheese
3 tablespoons chopped fresh parsley
1½ teaspoons anchovy essence
2-3 teaspoons lemon juice
5 eggs, separated
1 egg white
225 g (8 oz) mixed white and brown crabmeat
salt and pepper
2 tablespoons freshly grated Parmesan cheese
orange and fennel salad, to serve
marjoram sprigs, to garnish

Preheat oven to 200C (400F/Gas 6). Put a baking sheet to heat on lowest shelf. Butter a 2.25 litre (4 pint/2½ quart) soufflé dish. In a saucepan, melt butter, add onion and cook for 2-3 minutes. Stir in flour, cook for 1 minute, then gradually stir in milk. Bring to boil, stirring, then simmer gently for 4 minutes, stirring occasionally. Remove pan from heat and stir in soft cheese, chopped parsley, anchovy essence, lemon juice, egg yolks and crab and season with salt and pepper.

Whisk all the egg whites until stiff but not dry. Stir in 2 tablespoons crab mixture, then fold egg whites into remaining crab mixture in 3 batches. Transfer to soufflé dish, sprinkle Parmesan cheese over top and place dish on baking sheet. Bake for 40-45 minutes until lightly set in the centre. Serve immediately with orange and fennel salad, garnished with sprigs of marjoram.

Serves 4-6.

——— CAJUN CRABCAKES ———

1 small clove garlic, finely chopped
2 tablespoons finely chopped white and green parts
   spring onions
2 tablespoons finely chopped red pepper (capsicum)
1 egg, beaten
1½ tablespoons mayonnaise
450 g (1 lb) fresh white and brown crabmeat, chopped
1 tablespoon chopped fresh parsley
115 g (4 oz/2 cups) fresh breadcrumbs
squeeze lemon juice
salt and cayenne pepper
olive oil for shallow frying
sour cream and chopped chives and crisp green salad,
   to serve

Put garlic, spring onions, pepper (capsicum)
and a pinch salt in a mortar or small bowl and
crush together using a pestle or end of a
rolling pin. Stir in egg, mayonnaise, crabmeat, parsley and about half breadcrumbs to
bind together. Add lemon juice, salt and
cayenne pepper to taste.

Form crab mixture into 8 cakes 2 cm (¾ in)
thick and 6 cm (2½ in) round. Lightly press
in remaining breadcrumbs. Chill for 1 hour.
In a non-stick frying pan, heat a thin layer
oil, add crabcakes in batches and fry for 3-4
minutes on each side until golden. Serve
warm with sour cream and chives, and a crisp
green salad.

Makes 8.

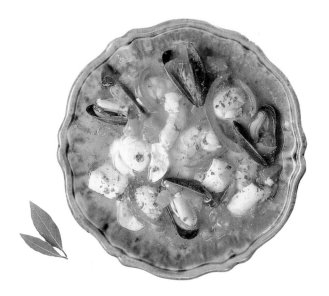

CIOPPINO

2 tablespoons light olive oil
1 large onion, chopped
3 cloves garlic, chopped
1 small red chilli, seeded and thinly sliced
1 red pepper (capsicum), seeded and sliced
575 g (1¼ lb) tomatoes
425 ml (15 fl oz/scant 1 cup) fish stock
115 ml (4 fl oz/½ cup) dry white wine
1 teaspoon dried oregano
1½ teaspoons each chopped fresh thyme and marjoram
1 bay leaf
225 g (8 oz) haddock, cod or halibut fillet, skinned
225 g (8 oz) large raw prawns
16 mussels, cleaned (see page 11)
4 large scallops, shelled (see page 11)
2½ tablespoons chopped fresh parsley

In a large, heavy-based saucepan, heat oil, add onion, garlic, chilli and pepper (capsicum) and cook gently until onion begins to colour. Meanwhile, peel, seed and chop tomatoes and add to pan with stock, wine and herbs, cover and simmer for 45 minutes.

Cut fish into cubes and peel prawns. Add mussels to pan, simmer for 1 minute, then add haddock, prawns and scallops. Cook over a low heat for 3-5 minutes until mussels have opened; discard any that remain closed. Sprinkle with parsley and serve at once.

Serves 4.

Note: Garnish with 8 unpeeled, cooked large prawns, if liked.

——————— STUFFED MUSSELS ———————

1 shallot, finely chopped
4 sprigs parsley
2 sprigs thyme
115 ml (4 fl oz/½ cup) dry white wine (optional)
1 kg (2 lb) mussels, cleaned (see page 11)
crusty bread, to serve
STUFFING:
1-2 cloves garlic, halved
4 sprigs parsley
leaves from 2 sprigs thyme
1 thin slice day-old bread
85 g (3 oz/¾ cup) unsalted butter
1 teaspoon grated lemon rind
2 teaspoons lemon juice
1¼ teaspoons Dijon mustard
salt and pepper

Put shallot, parsley and thyme in a large
saucepan with wine or 115 ml (4 fl oz/½ cup)
water and simmer for a few minutes, then add
mussels. Cover pan, bring to the boil and
cook mussels for 4-5 minutes, shaking pan
frequently, until shells open; discard any that
remain closed. Meanwhile, make stuffing.
Chop garlic and herbs together in a food
processor or blender. Remove crusts from
bread and add bread to food processor or
blender with butter, lemon rind and juice,
mustard and salt and pepper; set aside.

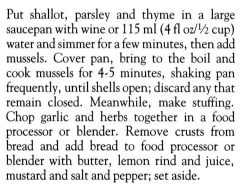

Preheat grill. Discard top shells from mussels.
Strain cooking juices and add 2-3 teaspoons
to stuffing to moisten it. Using a teaspoon,
spread a generous amount of stuffing on each
mussel, then place in a shallow baking dish.
Cook under grill for about 3 minutes until
golden and bubbling. Serve with plenty of
crusty bread.

Serves 2.

Note: Garnish with lemon and lime slices
and sprigs of parsley.

—MUSSELS IN TOMATO SAUCE—

2 tablespoons olive oil
2 shallots, finely chopped
2 cloves garlic, crushed
150 ml (5 fl oz/⅔ cup) medium-bodied dry white wine
250 g (9 oz) tomatoes, peeled, seeded and chopped
finely grated rind 1 lemon
2 tablespoons capers, chopped
3 tablespoons chopped fresh parsley
1.5 kg (3 lb) fresh mussels, cleaned
salt and pepper
crusty bread, to serve

In a large saucepan, heat oil, add shallots and garlic and cook gently until softened. Add wine, tomatoes, lemon rind, capers and half the parsley. Bring to the boil.

Add mussels to pan, cover and cook over a high heat for 3-4 minutes or until mussel shells have opened, shaking pan frequently; discard any mussels that remain closed. Season with salt and pepper, transfer to large bowls or soup plates, sprinkle over remaining parsley and serve with crusty bread.

Serves 2-3.

INDONESIAN STEAMED MUSSELS

1 kg (2 lb) mussels or clams, cleaned
7.5 cm (3 in) piece lemon grass, crushed and chopped
7.5 cm (3 in) piece fresh ginger, chopped
10 sprigs basil
torn basil leaves, to garnish
SWEET AND SOUR SAUCE:
400 g (14 oz) red peppers (capsicums), seeded and
    chopped
55 g (2 oz) fresh red chillies, seeded and chopped
3 cloves garlic, roughly chopped
4 tablespoons sugar
6 tablespoons vinegar
2 tablespoons olive oil
salt

To make sauce, put peppers (capsicums), chillies, garlic and 2 tablespoons water into a blender and purée. Transfer to a non-aluminium saucepan and add remaining sauce ingredients with 150 ml (5 fl oz/⅔ cup) water. Bring to the boil and simmer for 20 minutes or until reduced by half. Leave to cool, then transfer to a jar and refrigerate to allow flavours to develop. (It can be refrigerated for up to 2 weeks.)

Put mussels or clams, lemon grass, ginger and basil sprigs into a large saucepan and add sufficient water to come 4 cm (1½ in) up sides of pan. Bring to the boil, cover and cook over a moderate heat for 3-5 minutes until shells have opened; discard any that are closed. Meanwhile, transfer sauce to a small bowl. Drain mussels or clams, garnish with torn basil and serve with sauce.

Serves 4.

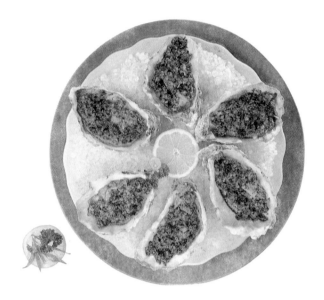

OYSTERS ROCKEFELLER

few handfuls rock salt
24 oysters, opened, on the half shell
115 g (4 oz/½ cup) butter
2 shallots, finely chopped
1 stick celery, finely chopped
225 g (8 oz) spinach, finely chopped
1 tablespoon chopped fresh parsley
1½ teaspoons chopped fresh tarragon
2 tablespoons fresh breadcrumbs
1 tablespoon Pernod or pastis
dash Tabasco sauce and Worcestershire sauce
salt and pepper

Spread a generous layer of rock salt over bottom of grill pan. Nestle oysters in salt.

In a saucepan or frying pan, heat a quarter of the butter, add shallots and celery and cook gently until softened but not coloured. Stir in spinach, parsley and tarragon and cook over a moderate heat until surplus moisture from spinach has evaporated.

Preheat grill. Purée spinach mixture in a blender, then mix in breadcrumbs, remaining butter, Pernod or pastis, Tabasco and Worcestershire sauces and season with salt and pepper. Place a tablespoonful of spinach mixture on each oyster and grill for about 3 minutes until beginning to turn golden. Serve at once.

Serves 4.

Note: Garnish with lemon slices and sprigs of parsley, if wished.

——ANGELS ON HORSEBACK——

4 bacon slices, rinds removed
8 oysters, shelled
4 slices bread
unsalted butter for spreading
pepper
lamb's lettuce and lemon twists, to garnish

Preheat grill. Cut each bacon slice across in half, then stretch each piece with the back of a knife. Wrap a piece of bacon around each oyster and place on a grill rack with ends of bacon underneath.

Toast bread, then place oysters under grill until crisp, turn over and crisp the other side.

Meanwhile, cut 2 circles from each slice of toast and butter circles. Place an oyster on each circle, grind over black pepper and serve garnished with lamb's lettuce and lemon twists.

Makes 8.

—— OYSTERS IN COFFINS ——

2 miniature brioche
55 g (2 oz/¹/₄ cup) unsalted butter, melted
6 large oysters
4 tablespoons sour cream
cayenne pepper and white pepper
finely grated lemon rind and slices, to garnish
tomato, onion and tarragon salad, to serve

Preheat oven to 220C (425F/Gas 7). Remove top knobs from brioche. Scoop out insides to leave a thin shell, taking care not to pierce walls. Brush brioches inside and out with half the melted butter. Place on a baking sheet and bake for 5-10 minutes until crisp.

Meanwhile, scrub oysters then, holding one at a time, curved side down in a cloth, prise open shells at hinge using a strong, short-bladed knife. Loosen each oyster and pour the liquid into pan with remaining melted butter. Boil for a few minutes until liquid is reduced then, over a low heat, add sour cream. Heat gently without boiling. Season with cayenne and white pepper.

Place 3 oysters in each brioche and pour the sauce over them. Garnish with lemon rind and slices and serve with tomato, onion and tarragon salad.

Serves 2.

—————— KEDGEREE ——————

575 g (1¼ lb) smoked haddock (finnan haddie)
  or salmon
115 g (4 oz/generous ½ cup) long grain rice
2 tablespoons lemon juice
150 ml (5 fl oz/⅔ cup) single (light) or sour cream
pinch of freshly grated nutmeg
cayenne pepper
2 hard-boiled eggs, peeled and chopped
55 g (2 oz/4 tablespoons) butter, diced
2 tablespoons chopped fresh parsley
parsley sprigs and sliced hard-boiled eggs, to garnish

Poach fish just covered by water for about 10 minutes. Lift fish from cooking liquid, discard bones and skin and flake flesh. Measure fish cooking liquid to twice volume of rice; top up with water if necessary. Bring to the boil, add rice, stir, then cover and simmer for about 15 minutes until rice is tender and liquid absorbed. Meanwhile, preheat oven to 180C (350F/Gas 4) and butter a baking dish.

Remove rice from heat and stir in lemon juice, cream, fish, nutmeg and a pinch of cayenne. Gently fold in eggs. Turn into dish, dot with butter and bake for about 25 minutes. Stir chopped parsley into kedgeree and garnish with parsley sprigs and sliced hard-boiled egg. Sprinkle a little cayenne pepper over the top, if wished.

Serves 4.

HADDOCK IN JACKET POTATOES

4 large baking potatoes, scrubbed and pricked
    with a fork
450 g (1 lb) smoked haddock (finnan haddie)
200 ml (7 fl oz/scant 1 cup) milk
2-3 teaspoons lemon juice
pepper
5-6 tablespoons sour cream or plain yogurt,
    preferably Greek style
2 tablespoons chopped fresh chives
1 tablespoon chopped fresh parsley
salad, to serve

Preheat oven to 200C (400F/Gas 6). Bake
the potatoes for 1½ hours until tender.

Meanwhile, put fish in a baking dish, pour
over milk, cover with greaseproof paper and
cook on bottom shelf in oven for about 8
minutes until flesh flakes. Drain fish,
reserving milk. Flake flesh finely, discarding
skin and bones, and season with lemon juice
and pepper. In a small bowl, mix sour cream
or yogurt with chives, parsley and pepper.

Cut a slice from top of each potato. Scoop out
most of insides of potatoes into a bowl, taking
care not to pierce skins. Beat potato insides
with reserved milk and pepper to taste, then
mix in the flaked fish. Spoon fish mixture
back into potato skins and spoon half the sour
cream or yogurt over the top. Return to oven
for about 10 minutes. Pour over the remaining cream or yogurt. Serve with salad.

Serves 4.

—OMELETTE ARNOLD BENNETT—

175 g (6 oz) smoked haddock (finnan haddie) fillet,
    poached and flaked
55 g (2 oz/4 tablespoons) butter, diced
175 ml (6 fl oz/³⁄₄ cup) whipping cream
4 eggs, separated
pepper
65 g (2½ oz/generous ½ cup) grated mature
    Cheddar cheese
lamb's lettuce, cress and lemon wedges, to garnish

Discard skin and bones from fish and flake
flesh. In a fairly small non-stick saucepan,
melt half the butter in 4 tablespoons cream,
then lightly stir in fish. Cover, remove from
heat and leave to cool.

Stir together egg yolks, 1 tablespoon cream
and pepper, then lightly stir in fish mixture.
Stir together cheese and remaining cream.

Preheat grill. Whisk egg whites until stiff but
not dry, then lightly fold into fish mixture in
3 batches. In an omelette pan, heat remaining butter. Pour in fish mixture and cook
until set and lightly browned underneath, but
still quite moist on the top. Pour cheese
mixture over the omelette, then grill until
golden and bubbling. Serve garnished with
lamb's lettuce, cress and lemon wedges.

Serves 2.

— SMOKED SALMON SCRAMBLE —

115 g (4 oz) smoked salmon trimmings, chopped
2 tablespoons single (light) cream
45 g (1½ oz/3 tablespoons) unsalted butter
4 large eggs, beaten
black pepper
chopped fresh chives and lime slices, to garnish
buttered toasted bagels, muffins or crumpets, to serve

In a small bowl, mix smoked salmon and cream together. Leave to stand for 10-15 minutes.

In a saucepan, melt half the butter, then stir in eggs. Cook over a low heat, stirring with a wooden spoon, until beginning to set. Add salmon and cream and season with pepper. Continue to stir until eggs are almost set.

Remove pan from heat and immediately stir in remaining butter. Garnish with chopped chives and lime slices and serve with buttered toasted bagels, muffins or crumpets.

Serves 2.

SALMON MILLE FEUILLES

175 ml (6 fl oz/¾ cup) plain yogurt, preferably
   Greek style, chilled
¾ teaspoon chopped fresh dill
salt and pepper
8 sheets filo pastry
melted butter
115 g (4 oz) smoked salmon trimmings, minced
2 tablespoons double (heavy) cream, chilled
1 bunch chives, roughly chopped
12 large slices smoked salmon
dill sprigs, to garnish
lemon wedges, to serve

Mix together half of yogurt with dill and salt
and pepper. Cover and chill. Preheat oven to
220C (425F/Gas 7). Cut twenty-four 7.5 cm
(3 in) circles from filo pastry. Lay half the
circles on a baking sheet, brush with melted
butter, then cover each circle with another.
Brush with melted butter and bake for 5
minutes until golden. Transfer to a wire rack
to cool. Put salmon trimmings in a blender
then, with motor running, slowly pour in
cream and remaining yogurt until just evenly
mixed. Add chives and pepper to taste.

Cut salmon into twelve 7.5 cm (3 in) circles.
Place pastry circle on a plate, spread with a
twelfth of the smoked salmon cream, then
cover with a smoked salmon circle. Repeat
twice more to make one mille feuille. Make
3 more mille feuille in the same way. Chill.
Serve garnished with dill sprigs and accompanied by sauce and lemon wedges.

Serves 4.

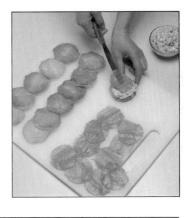

INDEX

Angels on Horseback, 113

Baked Bream with Fennel, 81
Baked Prawns & Courgettes, 96
Bass with Ginger & Lime, 51
Bream Dugléré, 80
Bream with Lemon & Herbs, 82
Bream with Tarragon, 48
Brill with Cardamom, 12

Cajun Crabcakes, 107
Cajun-Style Red Snapper, 91
Cantonese Prawns, 94
Ceviche, 44
Chinese Salad with Salmon, 65
Chinese-Style Bream, 83
Chowder, 27
Chunky Fish Casserole, 41
Cioppino, 108
Cleaning mussels, 11
Cod with Teriyaki Glaze, 30
Coulibiac, 62
Crab & Black Bean Sauce, 105
Crab Soufflé, 106

Escabeche, 90

Filleting fish, 10
Fish & Pesto Parcels, 20
Fish & Watercress Sauce, 79
Fish Cakes, 32
Fish Gratins, 33
Fish Plaki, 84
Fish with Mushroom Crust, 22

Goujons with Piquant Dip, 34
Gravad Lax, 68
Grilled Fish & Coriander, 45

Haddock in Jacket Potatoes,
116
Haddock & Parsley Sauce, 28
Haddock with Tomatoes, 29
Hake Baked with Potatoes, 46
Halibut with Paprika, 25
Halibut with Courgettes, 24

Herrings in Oatmeal, 73
Hot Fish Loaf, 35

Indian-Style Prawns, 97
Indonesian Steamed Mussels,
111

John Dory with Orange, 78

Kedgeree, 115

Layered Fish Terrine, 66
Lobster with Basil Dressing, 104

Mackerel with Mustard, 74
Mackerel with Yogurt, 75
Mediterranean Fish Soup, 102
Middle Eastern Monkfish, 40
Mixed Fish Pot, 58
Monkfish in Coconut Cream,
39
Monkfish on Ratatouille, 42
Mussels in Tomato Sauce, 110

Omelette Arnold Bennett, 117
Opening scallops, 11
Oysters in Coffins, 114
Oysters Rockefeller, 112

Peeling prawns, 11
Plaice with Prosciutto, 17
Prawns with Asian Sauce, 95

Red Snapper & Mushrooms, 92
Red Snapper with Crostini, 47
Roast Cod with Lentils, 31

Salmon Mille Feuilles, 119
Salmon Stir-Fry, 64
Salmon with Avocado Salsa, 60
Salmon with Herb Sauce, 61
Sardines in Coriander Sauce,
76
Scallop, Prawn & Mint Salad,
100
Sea Bass & Garlic, 50

Sea Bass Under a Crust, 49
Seafood Gumbo, 103
Sesame-Coated Whiting, 37
Shrimp Risotto, 98
Skate with Anchovy Sauce,
85
Skinning fish, 10
Smoked Salmon Scramble,
118
Sole with Chive Sauce, 15
Sole with Lettuce Filling, 16
Sole with Mint & Cucumber,
14
Spiced Bass, 52
Steamed Brill & Vegetables,
13
Stir-Fried Squid, 86
Stuffed Mussels, 109
Stuffed Sardines, 77
Stuffed Sole, 18
Stuffed Squid, 87
Swordfish with Sauce, 93
Swordfish with Tomatoes, 89

Tandoori Trout, 56
Thai Prawn & Noodle Soup,
101
Trout & Artichoke Frittata,
57
Trout with Hazelnuts, 54
Trout with Parma Ham, 55
Trout with Tomato Sauce,
53
Tuna & Ginger Vinaigrette,
72
Tuna Basquaise, 69
Turbot Parcels, 21
Turbot with Orange Sauce, 23
Turkish Swordfish Kebabs, 88

Warm Tuna Niçoise, 70
Whiting with Italian Sauce,
36
Whiting with Spinach, 38

Yogurt-Topped Halibut, 26